VITACOST.COM

WT27RJK83R
(14)

ISBN: 978-1-9163507-2-4 (paperback)
        978-1-9163507-3-1 (eBook)

Book cover design: Mary Ellen Sanger

Image credits: Mary Ellen Sanger and Karin Mlaker

Content development: 15 authors & Mary Ellen Sanger

Editor: Mary Ellen Sanger

Proof reader: David Fagan

Book design and layout: Vivechana Saraf, Soulscapes

For more information: www.soul-luxury.com
Enquiries: hello@soul-luxury.com

I AM
EVERY WOMAN

Trials, Tribulations, Triumphs and Discoveries:
a collection of extraordinary life journeys

15 AUTHORS

brought together by Claudia Roth

Your Guide to this Book

Introduction

    In My Own Words 7
    By Claudia Roth

Foreword

    Soul Conversations 9
    By Sarah Camilleri

Our Life Stories

1   *Abuse:* The Scars of Life 13
    By Louisa Pantameli

2   *Being true to myself:*
    The Risks and Rewards of a Curious Life 27
    By Justine Clement

3   *Brain tumour:* Titanium. 49
    By Julia Record

4   *Breaking tradition:*
    Trust That Whisper in Your Heart 63
    By Sharan Patel

5   *Burnout:* The Power of Pain 75
    By Karin Mlaker

6   *End of life:* Death... and Life 89
    By Susan Devine

7   *Family trauma:*
    Healing the Female Ancestral Line. 105
    By Stella Photi

8   *Feminine wisdom:* Evolving Beyond
    Perceptions of Gender 117
    By Uma Prajapati

9   *Finding my roots:*
    The Courage of Love, Faith and Hope........ 127
    By Liliana Martins

10 *Freedom:* Being Alive 139
    By Elodie Baran

11 *Heart condition:* Little Ballet Girl............. 151
    By Christine Hale

12 *Lifelong learning:*
    Learn to be a Chameleon.................... 165
    By Anja Loetscher

13 *Radical change:*
    My Luxury Life Was My Prison............. 177
    By Claudia Roth

14 *Seeking life's mission:* Transformation 191
    By Astrid Salas

15 *Self-love:* Honouring the Divine Mother
    is Honouring Yourself 205
    By Amanda Winwood

Write Your Own Story 217
    By Mary Ellen Sanger

Authors' Invitation........................... 225

Acknowledgements 226

In My Own Words

By Claudia Roth

The seed for the book that you are holding was planted back in the summer of 2019. Recovering from a major setback in my life, I found myself at a Mayan Wisdom Keepers' gathering in the middle of the English countryside surrounded by large trees. Mayans are indigenous people of Mexico and Central America. The wind was blowing and howling making the canvas of a large tipi tent flap relentlessly. The wooden tent poles rising high into the air stood firm, and a woman, a spiritual teacher, Jyoti (Jeneane Prevatt, PhD) was talking to a small group of us.

She had long, grey hair and was dressed in a white outfit, and as we all listened attentively something profound happened to me. I later understood that she had been not talking to me, as such, but to an older and wiser part of myself. Some people call this our Higher Self or Soul, but however you define it, the message landed. I found myself with a new kind of role model. Jyoti managed to completely turn on its head the way I look at life and growing older. Together we found a treasure – the woman inside of me who has wisdom, love and compassion that she longs to share.

It took a global pandemic for the seed of this book to sprout.

My need for conversation encouraged me to bring together a group of women. During the many gatherings we had, I surrendered to inner guidance, honouring my role of holding space for love, compassion and wisdom to emerge.

This book is an invitation to you to be inspired by 15 women's life stories stripped bare. I later found out that 15 is not just any number, but one of significance. The number 15 tells us we should listen to our intuition and wisdom, and use our many talents. 15 will help us reach our goals and release our fears.

My hope is that the stories of resilience, breaking free, finding inner peace and acceptance of the circle of life – birth, death and rebirth – will support you as you hold space for yourself and look at your own harvest, however difficult. When we meet challenges, we will rise above them and allow ourselves to grow.

You may be inspired to write your own life journey, as our authors did. It may be one of the most important steps toward self-discovery that you will ever make, for this kind of writing opens a path toward a clearer reflection of who you truly are and the meaning of life.

I am deeply grateful to all my teachers and spiritual mentors, including the amazing women – my co-authors – with whom I have shared many deeply transformative, precious, loving and empowering moments.

May you be empowered to stand in your truth,
Claudia

Soul Conversations

By Sarah Camilleri

The book you hold in your hands was crafted from many "soul conversations." It is a gift for you, lovingly put together by a group of remarkable women who formed a new "soul family" during the Covid-19 pandemic. These women, from all over the world and all walks of life, decided they wanted to share their collective wisdom about life, love and resilience. Each unique story has been written from the heart with the intention to help others – a gift to remind us all that we are not alone. This book aims to illuminate the pathway to self-compassion as well as the enormous power that human connection can bring.

How did it all begin? Right at the start of lockdown, I received an email from my good friend Claudia Roth, asking if I would join her and a few friends for a "Zoom coffee". I agreed without hesitation, before turning my attention back to the challenges of work and life as the world seemed to grind to a halt around me. This gentle invitation marked the start of a new journey of self-discovery for me as we met every Friday and shared time and wonderful, uplifting "soul conversations". As days stretched into months, I welcomed this weekly opportunity to connect with kindred spirits from all over the world.

As the world as we knew it rapidly retreated from view, we slipped our moorings and headed out into uncharted waters. Fear prevailed on every news channel and in conversation, and everything we regarded as constant began to shift or stop. In contrast to this darkness and uncertainty, we saw nature thrive and could more easily appreciate the majesty and sheer beauty of the world around us. As aeroplanes were grounded, we saw birds reclaim the skies, singing that little bit louder, as if celebrating a new and unexpected dawn.

The pandemic also shone a light onto the enduring human desire for connection and positivity. Importantly, in some profoundly still moments that lockdown brought, we began to fully contemplate our lives, what really matters and how invaluable love, connection and human touch is to us all.

Claudia's intuition to bring us together at this time was a gift, anchoring us and helping us to reflect, recharge and get ready for the week ahead. Our meetings provided a safe harbour in which to tap into the extraordinary energy of our new "soul family". Our conversations were transformational and flowed like water as if from the source. We shared meditations, life stories and experiences of how our worlds seemed to be shifting from stillness to a new era of consciousness.

This collection of stories was one of the great ideas to emerge from our Coffee Morning conversations and has been transformative and cathartic for all of our authors. If you have ever been taken off your familiar path by crisis or hardship, had your bravery and resilience tested, or made bold changes in your path to live life more fully, this book has been written for you. We hope some of the knowledge and life stories told in this beautiful volume will resonate with you and help you on your own quest for self-love, healing and mastery of this precious gift called "life".

We would also like to invite you to write your own story or

life-changing chapter, one that your loved ones and their loved ones may one day read and take courage and inspiration from. You can find some guidance on writing your own story at the end of this book. We invite you to reach out to us. We all hang out on a private Facebook page – we started by sharing and we hope the sharing continues!

With support and love for all – women and men – we can thrive and take an invitation from the Divine to hold space for each other and help lift the conversation higher for future, more enlightened generations. It is up to us to write the inspirational stories from our lives and share as we are able, to ensure that the power of love, discovery and human connection is ever-present as we bring more wellness and healing to our beautiful world.

Be well,
Sarah Camilleri
Founding editor
European Spa magazine

The Scars of Life

By Louisa Pantameli

The Scars of Life

*"It took me 33 years to leave an abusive relationship.
We survive. We resurrect."*

Prologue: A golden journey
When the Japanese mend broken objects, they accentuate the
damage by filling the cracks with gold. They believe that when
something has suffered damage and has a history, it becomes
more beautiful.

The more I talk with people, the more I realise we are all broken, but often we mend in the most miraculous ways: we survive, we resurrect, we reinvent ourselves. Best of all, given time,
we learn to love ourselves just the way we are and thus let ourselves be loved, just the way we are. We are all beautiful.

My children and I carry the scars of abuse and survival. Like
the cracks in the Japanese objects filled with gold, our scars are
our history and they make us who we are.

Whatever you need to do, you'll do when you are ready
It took me 33 years and bringing up two children to leave an
abusive relationship. Thirty-three years!

My daughter and I left on Friday, November 25, 2016: The
International Day for the Elimination of Violence Against

Women. The timing wasn't intentional. I didn't even know that such a day existed, but looking back it seems appropriate that we took our first step towards freedom then.

Except for some clothing and text books, we left everything behind that had once seemed important: a father, a husband, a dog, a cat, an eight-bedroom property with its tennis court, swimming pool, stables, furniture and all our private possessions. In short, we left everything we knew behind and took our first step into the unknown.

My daughter and I moved into rented accommodation smaller than our previous kitchen. I was 53 and I hadn't earned money in two decades. I had been with my husband for 33 years, 27 of those married. My son was 21 and in his last year at university and my daughter was 17 and in her last A-level year.

I cried when I tried to cook our first meal in our new home. Everything was new and different. I had nothing: no cooking utensils, no spices, none of the things one accumulates over a lifetime and that one takes for granted. I gave myself a stern talking-to and reminded myself that millions of people live with less, that we were fortunate.

We sat at the kitchen table eating our first simple dinner in our new home.

'Mami, I am so happy,' my daughter said.

'That is so lovely,' I replied. 'What made you say that?'

'I am no longer stressed,' she explained. 'I didn't realise before how stressed I was, but now I have a real sense of peace.'

At that very moment, I knew that whatever hardships the next few years would throw at us, it would be worth it. We had taken our first step; we were on our way and one day we would be free.

Pain passed from generation to generation

My parents came from rather different backgrounds. My mother was born in the countryside during World War Two. Her father was a successful architect, but her parents lost everything during the war: a daughter, their home, their freedom and their livelihoods. My grandmother never got over the death of her child and was not able to love my mum the way she deserved. My mum never felt she was as pretty, as clever, as good or as worthy as the sister she had never met. After the war, my grandfather managed to build back his practice and provide a very comfortable living for his family.

My father was already eight when the war started. Abandoned by his father, his mother had no time to love and look after him the way he deserved, as she was busy running a pub to support them both. He roamed the streets of war-torn Berlin, fending for himself, picking up cigarette butts and learning to speak English from the soldiers.

My mother went to a finishing school in Switzerland and had just started her first job when she met my father, who was ten years older than her. It was a whirlwind romance and she soon got pregnant with me, bleeding until they got married three months later. My mother's parents did not approve of the marriage.

I wonder whether we can be born with angst already embedded in our DNA? Can we exit the womb feeling unloved or that we are not enough unless our circumstances or we are perfect? It sometimes seems that decades of pain can be passed down from generation to generation.

Seen but not heard

I was born in Germany, the eldest of three girls. I always thought I had a normal childhood, one of freedom from the pressures that many young people face nowadays. I wasn't aware of my eyebrows until well into my 20s, nor did I think about my tummy, my bottom or the length of my legs; they just were what they were.

My sisters and I roller-skated, cycled and roamed the streets with our neighbours. Then in 1973 we moved to a Spanish island. Franco was still alive and there were no other foreigners on the island. Most of the inhabitants were subsistence farmers and we spoke no Spanish. I was ten and I was excited. It was an adventure. My father wanted "the good life", away from car fumes and pesticides and industrialisation. My mother loved the city, she didn't want to move to an island, but we did what my father wanted.

Looking back, we always did what my father wanted and we all did what was necessary to keep him happy and to keep the peace. He was an interesting and interested man, but the world revolved around him and as children we knew exactly where our place was. We knew not to anger him. We knew not to ask for things. We knew that if we were allowed to step out for lunch with my parents, we had to behave. There was no running around, complaining about food or moaning. The alternative was simply that we would be left home alone.

My father would return to Germany regularly to get his culture fix, while my mother was stuck in the mountains with three children under the age of ten. We were left unsupervised most of the time, as long as we didn't cause trouble and we were back for German dinner time. We had horses and rode to the beach and went swimming in the Atlantic Ocean. We walked along the canal from morning to night, swam in water tanks, explored abandoned houses and found treasures.

This was before mobile phones, before parents dedicated all their time to their offspring. If we wanted to get somewhere we had to ride, walk or hitchhike there. We played cards with the children who came from subsistence farming households, bounced a tennis ball off a wall for hours on end, fed baby mice, watched puppies being born and goats and pigs slaughtered. We learned Spanish and we went to the local school.

My parents never fought, but then one day, when I was 15, we were called into the living room and told that they were going to get divorced. It turned out that my father got way more than a culture fix when he went to Germany. Seemingly, even before we left he had been free with his favours. My mum was only 35 and felt she didn't know her husband. She wanted a divorce.

We moved into a house in the main town while my father stayed in the mountains. Every weekend we had to visit him. We were now teenagers and preferred to be in town so we could see our friends and go out and have fun. Spending every weekend on a farm in the mountains wasn't our idea of a good time. Our mum begged us, as she would feel his wrath if we didn't go. So, we spent our weekends in the mountains with our father. He was always angry during those last three years I was at home. I left the island the very day I turned 18.

I thought we had been free and had an easy childhood, but looking back, trying to make sense of what happened later in my life, I realise we weren't free. We did what my father wanted. If he was angry everybody would tiptoe around the house. If he was happy then everyone could breathe easy. My mother did what my father wanted. She was not a rebel. In fact, the most rebellious things she ever did were to marry and divorce my father.

Normalising insanity
After my secondary education in Spain, I spent a year in London as an au pair and a year at a university in Germany, ending up at a university in England. I met my future husband on my first day there. Even though he had finished his degree the previous year,

he was playing in a band and knew one of the girls I was living with. He invited us all to come and see him perform. We went to see his gig and the rest is history.

I finished my degree and helped to set up our first company. I worked all day, cleaned and cooked in the evening, and spent the weekends alone as he played golf or rehearsed with his band. After five years I decided that I had had enough, so I left and went to Germany to work in an advertising agency. Suddenly the man who had no time for me while I was in England found hours and hours of time to pursue me daily.

Eventually, I relented and agreed to go back to England. His conditions were that we buy a house together, get married immediately, and own our assets jointly. At the time, I thought that was love. We married, we worked, and at 32 I had my first child. But when we sold our first company, the money went into his account. His insistence on joint ownership disappeared and I received an allowance. Then another baby arrived.

The physical violence started early on. He was always angry. Nothing I did was enough. I wasn't thin enough, tidy enough. If I agreed, I was uninteresting; if I disagreed, I was picking a fight. I was trapped in a lose-lose situation. I slept in the spare bedroom with the baby, as he needed his sleep to be able to work. His job, of course, was more important than mine and I eventually gave up my career. I couldn't do it all: run the house, look after the baby, support my husband. He controlled the money.

I went into a kind of deep slumber. I lost myself. I barely functioned. He now controlled all aspects of my life: I had two babies, no money and no job. He had made sure I could not escape again, but more importantly, I felt I could not escape.

Nobody marries an abuser, they marry a façade. The abuser hooks you and slowly reels you in. Once they have fully landed you, the game starts. A game of carrots and sticks, of gaslighting, until in the end you no longer know what is right or wrong. You start to doubt yourself. You question your own judgement. You question your own reality.

He was an interesting man, I thought to myself, he was ambitious and entertaining. I must have done something to make him angry. It must be my fault. Once upon a time he was nice to me, he pursued me and wanted me. Surely, if only I could change, everything would be better.

It was the 1990s and 2000s, and nobody I knew talked about domestic violence, coercive control, or financial control. But I did hear about social services taking children away from "dysfunctional" families. I was petrified to call the police. I didn't want to lose my children. They were all that mattered to me. Solicitors I talked to could not reassure me of the outcome. It would be up to a judge to decide whether the children would stay with me or my husband. I simply could not take that risk.

When I told my father that my husband hit me, he replied that he, too, would hit me. I was gutted. It surely was my fault. I wasn't obedient enough. I didn't do what was necessary to keep a man happy. So, I stayed and tried to make our life as safe as possible.

I normalised this insanity. I made excuses so my brain could cope with what was happening and somehow make sense out of what didn't make sense. Humans are very good at making the abnormal seem normal, creating stories to cope with what should be unbearable. I didn't know how to leave.

As the children grew up, they observed daily life in friends' homes and realised that our household was far from normal. We always spoke about it and I made no allowances. I explained that our situation might be wrong, but that right now I was doing the best I could.

You can only change yourself

Finally, I went to a counsellor to try and make sense of my life. The main lesson I took from those sessions was that you can only change yourself, and when you change, your environment will change too. When you have hiked up a mountain, you can either go back to where you came from or look down into the next valley and descend into the unknown.

My journey to freedom didn't start when he put spyware on my computer. Or when he came at me with a knife while I held our daughter in my arms. It didn't start when he pinned me against the kitchen cupboard during my pregnancy, or when he put my head through the wall in front of our daughter and I broke my wrist. It didn't start, either, when I couldn't move my arm because it was so bruised, or when he tried to drown me, or when he punched me in the face and broke my glasses, or when he destroyed my possessions in a fit of rage. It started when I broke my back.

We were on a family coasteering activity, jumping from high rocks into the water. The first jump was high enough for me and the second seemed too high. The young people had already jumped and I hesitated. My husband was behind me. You had to jump in feet first with your arms by your side so that your feet would break the water. The guide said to just take a run at it, so I did, ignoring my inner voice.

As I landed, bottom first, I felt my lower vertebrae meet my upper vertebrae half way and immediately knew something serious had happened. I sustained compression fractures of several vertebrae and squished a few discs. Nothing could be done about it. As my GP so charmingly said: 'At your age, you start to stoop forwards anyway.'

In that moment, I woke from my slumber. I regained consciousness. I realised that only I was responsible for my life and only I could make it better. That was the beginning. I started "hiking up that mountain." I started working on myself.

First, I healed my back by swimming through tears of pain and with help from a sports masseur to ensure that I didn't seize up. I also lost weight, then once I could move again without pain, I decided to get fit and took up running. I was 50 and had never in my life been a runner. I started by walking one step and running one step, then running two steps, then three. Then one day I could run a whole mile on the flat. I started running up little hills. Soon, with the help of my sister, I ran my first 5k for a cancer charity. I had achieved what had seemed impossible to me not that long ago.

My body was healing. I was physically fit and my soul started to heal and get stronger, too. I found my light, my energy, and discovered it to have a teenage vitality, scattered all over the place. My son calls it my 'chaotic energy' and I am still working on getting it focused. But I had begun testing my strength and finally, I was taking care of myself.

You already know what you need to do

As I grew stronger I needed to decide whether to look back and return to where I came from or to go down the other side of the mountain and into the unknown.

As so often happens in life, at the time I "coincidentally" saw an advertisement for a female life coach. She was a gorgeous, spiritual woman who believed in astrology and numerology and energy and healing waves. I told nobody about her. My friends would have thought that I had finally lost it. It was a completely new world for me. I felt embraced and safe. Our discussions weren't so much about rational thoughts but about feelings, something I had tried to suppress for quite some time.

Do I leave or do I stay? What should I do? We spent hours

and hours deliberating. One day she said to me: 'You already know what it is you need to do.' It's funny how such a simple sentence can carry so much power. She was right. I knew what to do, although it would take another two years until I took any real action.

Fear stands for "false evidence appearing real"
In the first year after we left, I dedicated my time entirely to my daughter just finishing her A-levels, and my son in university.

I cut up strawberries and nectarines and washed grapes to feed my daughter, got her to exercise, and kept her environment as cool, calm and collected as possible, so she could fully concentrate on her A-levels. She worked hard, got fabulous results and secured a place at her first choice of university.

At the same time, I made sure my son did well at university. He graduated nearly a year later and came to live with me in my 2.5-bedroom rented property. I let him do exactly what he wanted for two months, which meant spending hours on end playing computer games, but when my daughter went to university, I told him it was time for him to spread his wings and get out into the big wide world.

A month after he went off travelling, it was time to confront my own reality. I was like a rabbit in the headlights. Fear had paralysed me. I was now 54 years old and I hadn't earned money in over two decades. All the money was still in my husband's name and he had made it quite clear that he would give me nothing. I knew it was going to be a long and tough battle and I knew he had the resources, the energy and the desire to fight me every step of the way. Was I strong enough to fight a man who had controlled me and kept me down for such a long time?

Fortunately, the universe sent another person to help me. We walked and talked and she recommended the book *The Chimp*

Paradox by Professor Steve Peters. As I worked my way through it, I realised that fear was stopping me from living. I was freezing, hoping all would go away. Fear is an emotion about a future that hasn't happened yet, and might never happen. I was paralysed in the present. Fear makes your inner chimp (your subconscious) naughty and restless, and it controls all your actions. I needed to calm my "inner chimp". I started feeding it bananas to stop it screaming. I exercised it lots so it would go to sleep. And one day my "chimp" and I had the strength to start my journey again.

I hired a solicitor, served divorce papers and got a mortgage to buy a place that we could make our own. I went on holidays by myself, climbed Mount Snowdon in Wales, got a coaching qualification and made new friends. I realised I needed to continue living, moving forward and growing. Each day I am grateful I took that first step. I am no longer frightened. I have discovered an inner strength that I didn't know I had, which had lain dormant within me.

Not quite the end
It's been a long, long journey and after four years, I am still controlled financially and emotionally by the man I left. So, the journey to freedom isn't over. But I keep breathing and reminding myself that this, too, shall pass, that it is okay to cry when I am overwhelmed and to rest when I am tired. I am amazed at how far we have come and I am eternally grateful to my family and friends who have supported and at times carried me.

The last four years have been scary and exhausting, yet they have been the happiest of our lives. We are healing, growing, safe and cocooned in our new home. My son said to me not long ago: 'I am not upset by the things that have happened to me. They make me who I am.'

My children and I carry the wounds of abuse and survival, but like the cracks in the Japanese objects filled with gold, our scars are our history and they make us who we are. We are able to mend in the most miraculous ways. We survive. We resurrect. We reinvent ourselves. Best of all, given time, we learn to love ourselves just the way we are, letting ourselves be loved, just the way we are.

The Risks and Rewards
of a Curious Life

By Justine Clement

The Risks and Rewards
of a Curious Life

*"There were actually other people like me!
All at once I felt more normal, more accepting
of myself. All I needed was to trust."*

I am often to be found here, by the sea. It's where I feel at home, where I feel connected and where I sit now, to write this story. I grew up by water. Not just the sea, but near a magical, sacred and ancient spring called St Piran's Well, in a small village mid-way between the spectacular north and south Cornish coastlines. Weekends were spent with my parents and sister, walking some of the hundreds of rugged paths that dot the shorelines. During the week, I would spend much of my time playing in our garden where, running along the boundary between us and the farmer's fields, there was a stream that was the perfect size for little people to play, splash and stomp about in. We were, and still are, an active, outdoors and energetic kind of family.

We're Celtic. Welsh to be precise. I like saying that because I've recently begun reconnecting to my roots. My dad recently asked me why, 15 or so years ago, when someone questioned where I was from, I replied, 'I'm not from anywhere.' I tried to explain to him that I have spent what feels like a lifetime of not quite knowing my place in the world, not quite *feeling* my roots. My mother and father, on the other hand, feel Welsh to their cores. Born in Wales to Welsh-born parents, except my maternal grandfather, who was an orphan, they met in their early 20s while working for an insurance broker near Swansea in South Wales. My mother always told me how much she loved it there at her first real job. But in those days, just one generation ago, couples who got together from within the same office weren't allowed to remain working alongside each other, and it was always the woman who was asked to leave.

Despite having always known about this, it still sits uneasily with me even now. It's utterly irrational, I know, but in some way I feel guilty, as if in being a product of their marriage I've been partly responsible for some of my mother's pain. I feel the same uneasiness about the fact that it wasn't until 1975, five years after I was born, that women in Britain were allowed to open their own bank accounts. I feel guilty for having benefitted from all the sacrifices women before me have had to make, and I'm not sure what I've done to thank them or repay them. It troubles me, but it also allowed me live my life without considering I was a woman – the underdog, the unequal. As a result, there have only been a few occasions when this has ever been a problem for me. Perhaps that is my payment back to these women – a show of progress, in some small way.

A childhood of adventure

My early years were spent in Wales and then, when I turned three and my sister was eight, my father accepted a new job and we all headed off on a big adventure to Cornwall. We arrived at a house that my father had rented in the middle of nowhere, which came complete with a resident rat and was surrounded by damp woodland. It was not an easy first few years away from home for my mother, left alone during the day with two young children and nowhere to go without a car.

After a few years, they had saved enough for their first house. Riding my bike to the little village school just a mile down the road, I flourished. I was quite sporty, had friends and did reasonably well with my schoolwork. There is nothing remarkable in the story. While we had abandoned our Welsh roots, it was a happy childhood in Cornwall. The worst complaint I had was wishing my mum, like the others, would visit me more at the school gate, bringing me a liquorice treat and some of her love. But it wasn't her fault; unlike the other mums, she was always at work and that meant sometimes being late to pick me up. But I adored her and in those early years when I wasn't at school, I'd spend much of my time helping her bake bread, make jams and chutneys, and eating the cake mixture while she wasn't looking.

Evenings and weekends meant messing about outside in the garden and the stream with friends. I'd help – and hinder – my parents as they built dry stone walls, and I had my own little patch of garden to grow vegetables. I would spend hours crushing rose petals to make perfume and come back, laden with buckets full of fool's gold I'd found beneath the nearby viaduct. Precious and shimmering, how I adored collecting those stones. Having sociable parents was fun, too, and I loved hearing the sound of their dinner parties going on downstairs as they danced to Elvis and Brazilian bands. The house was alive, and so were we.

'I'm going to ask Father Christmas for a wigwam and a feather headdress,' I announced one year. One other winter, I asked for a Lone Ranger, complete with a white plastic horse and his friend Tonto. The best present I ever received, though, was the red Grifter bike I found waiting on the stairs one year. Forty-two years later, I can still recall the excitement of seeing it for the first time. But my all-time favourite toy was a little plastic farm in a box. How I loved building the little hedges and deciding which animals or flocks would go into each section. I would take it out again and again, never getting bored with it.

I'm not sure anyone thought too much about it at the time, but I was most certainly a tomboy. One year, I decided to break the mould and ask for a pram, but after two days I was utterly bored of it and went back to my beloved bike. I hated shopping and hated dresses even more. What felt like one of the worst days of my young life was playing the role of bridesmaid at a family friend's wedding. It felt like such a cruel punishment, to have to wear a frilly dress and have my hair crimped. My indignation shows in every picture taken that day. I wanted to be out roaming the hills, swimming in the sea, riding my bike and having adventures with my friends. I was curious and passionate about life and wanted to do it all, see it all, feel it all.

Was I different to all my friends in those early days? I didn't think so and I'm not sure anyone else did. Things were generally different back then, far less open and with far fewer options to consider. It wasn't until much later that it all became clearer to me, and to us all.

My teenage years were no doubt fraught at times, just like anyone else's, but I loved working in my dad's sports shop, talking to people from all walks of life. It was a family affair and even my grandparents would sometimes make the six-hour journey from Wales to come and help out. Eventually we added a gym and a little spa to the back of the shop. It wasn't grand, but it was different for the times, and it was fun. Christmas would be spent with all three generations sitting in the hot tub and sauna. I wasn't embarrassed by my parents like most teenagers. I felt proud of them and what they'd achieved, and grateful for the life they'd worked hard to give us.

Indeed, the older I get, the more I feel grateful for what my parents, grandparents and older sister did for me over the years. It's easy to become complacent and ungrateful – you see this in people everywhere. It's easy to blame others for what has not happened or what's gone wrong instead of remembering what has happened and what went right. It's easy to forget all the sacrifices other people have made for you. I have realised that life is harder without gratitude, but it's something I've had to consciously practice and consider each and every day. Gratitude is something I consider the moment I wake up and right before I go to bed. It can be easy to take both the little and the big things for granted; having a cosy bed to sleep in, loving and being loved, even life itself. Without this practice, when life gets tough, as inevitably it does, things can become clouded, others can be blamed and life is easily thrown out of balance and joy.

Broadening horizons
'I didn't get in,' my friend protested as she burst forth the news that had just arrived through the 'letterbox of doom,' as she'd called it that day. I was so sad for her. We'd been a team up until then; just a month earlier she excitedly told me that summer camps for rich kids in America were looking for people just like us to go and work for them. It was the first time I'd ever heard of such a thing and I could feel a burst of excitement welling up inside me. We were 18 and just finishing our A levels. But a week later, when my letter arrived, the news for me was altogether more positive. I'd been accepted to teach tennis to affluent Jewish-American children in upstate New York. I couldn't believe my luck, but I also felt guilty that I was going and my dear friend was not.

Luck aside, from the moment we opened that letter my father, mother and I all knew, somewhere deep inside us, that it would also herald my first steps towards leaving home. With excitement also came nerves, but within a matter of few weeks my dad was driving me up to Heathrow. I worked hard to appear utterly mature and cover up a rising feeling of trepidation. I could feel it effervescing under my carefully chosen "Big American Adventure" outfit, and I did everything I could to make sure it didn't escape into the confines of our lime green Vauxhall Astra.

Thinking back, like most teenagers, it was no doubt all about "me". Yet knowing now that my leaving home hit my mother hard, I feel so sad to think of her at home alone that day, realising a new chapter would be unfolding for her, too. Business books tell you that empathy is one of the most important traits of a great CEO. I say it's one of the most important traits in any human being. Empathy gives life more colour, greater depth and more meaning, and it makes you a better person.

Life for me has always been – and still is – a series of big, yet sometimes scary adventures, but ones that need to be lived, regardless. I suppose, thinking about it now, that's one of my guiding principles: Explore the world in the company of good people. It's certainly a thought that makes my heart sing. It fills me up with love, joy and admiration and I feel utterly complete and at one with the world.

I was still in America, having a ball, when Dad called me one day to cautiously give me some news.

'I've got you a place,' he told me. 'At a polytechnic in Bournemouth. If you fancy it, love?'

I wasn't sure I did. Rather, I felt a bit miffed and annoyed that he'd taken charge of the next chapter of my life. He knew it too. But after some persuasion on his part and some consideration on mine, guiding principle number two came into play in my life: Be grateful to those who sometimes know you better than you know yourself.

We both knew my grades were incredibly average because, for some unknown reason, while my parents presumed I had been upstairs working hard and revising, I had actually been snoozing for some of the time. Why I'd chosen economics as one of my subjects will forever be puzzling to all of us. John Maynard Keynes and his ideas were, and will forever remain, a complete mystery to me. In a few weeks the big American adventure would be over and I'd be returning home with no plans and no idea what I wanted to do with my life. A day later, I called my dad back. 'Let's do it,' I said.

An Italian adventure

In a very short space of time I was indeed incredibly grateful to my dad, because college was a hugely influential period of my life. It was a time of growing up, of insecurity, of learning, of passion and ultimately, of discovering the many parts of who I really was. Yet, like so many periods of my life, I didn't realise it at the time. I never stopped to consolidate, to consider, to think or to reflect. So much happened during those years that to say they were formative would be an understatement.

I took jobs to help pay my way, at times having three different places to go to in a single day. I went from carrying out chambermaid duties to working in admin at an incredibly dour insurance company before cycling miles to operate the lipstick machine at the Revlon factory. It all helped fund those years. My parents' business did well but we were never wealthy; always careful and working hard to pay for the lives we wanted to live.

Boys came and went – lots of them – but no one ever seemed quite right. I'd flit from one to another, focused on looks, but it was always a bit hollow and for some reason I had little respect for any of the boys I went out with. To me, spending time with my friends always seemed more interesting. I just wanted to have fun, or so I told myself at the time.

'Have you seen The Lady magazine this week?' my friend called me excitedly one evening.

'No, why?' I replied.

'There's a job advertised that's just made for us, it will be such fun!'

She could not have been more right. After finishing my studies in Bournemouth, my friend suggested we go on an adventure together to Italy, where we would work as au pairs for two families. My job was to look after two boys aged seven and ten. Despite having no experience whatsoever, I thought, 'why not?' But just as we were about to leave, my friend pulled out. Unlike me, she had fallen in love. So, off I went again on my own, arriving to meet my host family on the shores of Lake Garda, complete with little more than a smile and a bundle of skis from my dad's sports shop.

I was going purely on instinct, I guess, as I had no real idea who I would be working for. Except for a few phone calls, I hadn't dug too deeply into the details. I'm often reminded that this is a trait of mine. For me, life's too short to spend too much time on detail. Even then I was happier to go on my intuition. If it felt right and it excited me, then I should just say "yes".

The mother of the family picked me up at the airport, laughing at my outdated skis and English outfit of light trousers and T-shirt in the depths of a northern Italian winter. Everyone else was quilted up with the latest and, of course, most stylish ski jackets. She drove me back to their home, down a long, beautiful valley road lined with cypress trees. Suddenly, appearing out of the mist, was one of the most spectacular villas I have ever seen, standing right on the edge of the lake. I'd landed on my feet, I told myself, working for a Count and a Countess who lived on what was surely one of the most stunning estates in Italy.

However, true to form, within a few days I'd already got myself into trouble.

'Let's go!' I yelled over to the youngest boy, aged seven, both of us brimming with excitement at the snow that had started to fall. 'Where are the biggest slopes around here?'

'Over there,' he yelped back at me with elation.

'This one is fun,' he must have thought to himself upon my arrival in their house. Neither of us gave a second thought to the broken arm he'd suffered playing football with his brother a few days before I arrived. Minutes later we were roly-polying down a snow-covered hill, one after the other, collapsing into giggles, sodden yet elated. The only problem was that I'd completely forgotten he was supposed to be back at school that afternoon. We were jolted back into reality when, in the distance, we heard his mother shouting angrily for him.

We looked at each other anxiously and somewhat confused for a minute or two before the Countess eventually caught up with us. She was not happy with me, not happy at all. Forthwith came my first of many huge Italian-style rollickings I received on that trip. Standing there, supposed to be an adult with a new role and all the responsibilities that came with it, I felt ashamed and foolish. What was I thinking? At the time, both of us probably wondered whether I was really cut out for the job, but in some of the many conversations we've had since then, she confided that she had been secretly laughing her head off at the scene played out before her.

Instead of the planned six-month adventure, I spent almost three years with my new family. Every time I thought it might be time to leave and head back to "real life," they would make every effort to persuade me stay. I was happy there and Britain was also in the grip of a recession, so friends told me there was little point in returning.

Month-long summers, sometimes longer, were spent in Tuscany on the beach with the family and new au pair friends that I had made. On my one day off a week, I would venture off with a friend to nearby islands and because we were broke, we'd find a boat to sleep under on the beach. Years later we would travel together to Cuba. That was in the days when the country was still very much closed to tourists, and a young man in a wide-brimmed hat and rubber boots beckoned us from a street corner.

'Hey, over here? Wanna come horse-riding?' he called out, explaining that he could offer us a horseback adventure into the sugar cane fields. My friend vigorously shook her head.

'No way,' she said, 'I'm not going with him'

'Aw, come on,' I said, 'it will be an adventure.'

Eventually we set off, she on her trusty steed, Papahito, and me trotting behind wearing a large grin. We had the most incredible day, bathing in freshwater pools and eating raw sugar cane plucked from the fields. But it only happened because we'd said "yes".

The Italian family is still very much a part of my life all these years later. We've shared life's ups and downs and my life has been immeasurably richer for having said "yes" to that experience. So here comes my next guiding principle: When crossroads and opportunities appear in your life that sound like fun, just say "yes". It's wise to be cautious, of course, but don't let that stop you taking calculated risks. Hone your intuition and go for it! Don't let fear stop you, because you just never know where the path may take you. Follow your curiosity; don't shy away due to fear of failure, rejection or the unknown. My life, thus far, has proven to me that despite being scared at times, it's always worth taking those risks.

London calling

'I'm sorry, but I have to go this time, for sure.' I told the Countess.
There came a point when I knew change was needed and I eventually felt brave enough to tell my Italian family that I would
definitely be leaving them this time. I knew I was instigating a
massive change not just for me, but for all of us, and I felt incredibly guilty about going, but I knew I had to follow through.
This was becoming a restrictive life and one that did not feel as
though it were my own; living in a lovely, but dark little bedroom
off the kitchen. So, I said "yes" to moving to London with two
British friends I'd met in Verona. Having only ever been to London once before, it felt exciting and daunting to go there, find a
proper job and share a house with four others.

What followed over the next few years was a series of great
adventures as well as scrapes and initiations into the harsh real-
ities of inner-city living. That first house was burgled, twice.
Once, it turned out, by a serial rapist who'd climbed in through a
ground-floor bedroom window and stolen an ornamental sword
from the boyfriend of one of my roommates. Only a week earlier, I'd moved out of that very room to start a new job in the
Alps. We were later told by police that the sword was "Exhibit
A" in his subsequent trial for the rape of nine women in the area.

On another occasion, one night I was walking home in the
depths of winter, down a dark dingy street not far from my
rented flat in Brixton. I had my heavy coat wrapped tightly about
me for warmth and was carrying what felt like my world in my
laptop, when I caught sight of a man kicking what looked like
a mountain of rubbish out of an old car. I walked hurriedly by,
but before I could pass he came up behind me and placed a large
knife to my throat.

'Give me your f***ing money,' he growled into my ear. There
was no way out. Cautiously, I dropped my precious laptop into

the shadows, hoping he wouldn't notice.

'Fine,' I said. 'I'll give you what I have, but there's no point in you taking my bank cards, they're of no use to you.'

Chip and pin wasn't around in those days and he most likely knew I'd cancel them the minute I got away. I have no idea how I kept my composure and managed to talk my way out of trouble that night. I even managed to pick up my precious laptop without him noticing, but by the time I got home, the shock of the experience suddenly overwhelmed me and the tears flooded out. I cried for hours and hours and the tears just kept falling. I loved London, but I also felt truly sorry for myself, a victim, and fed up with the dangers of edgy urban life.

Unfortunately my brushes with criminality didn't finish there. Just a few months later, the entire contents of my flat were stolen; unashamedly carted out in broad daylight through the front door. While I loved living in that exciting part of London, I was growing weary of all the violence, looting and loss.

A defining moment

In amongst all this, I played around with jobs, mostly in travel, working for small companies that attracted my curiosity. Looking back, I realise they were mostly run by women, but I didn't appreciate how unusual that was at the time. I did a stint at an Italian opera agency, another working as a letting agent, one for an Egyptian tour operator and diving specialist, and along the way I made friends and had more great adventures. Travelling had become my love and any chance I could get, I was off, arranging holidays and exploring the world with friends. Hiring an Egyptian felucca and sailing down the River Nile was a highlight. We'd sleep out on deck at night with the stars as our canopy and only the Nubian captain's donkey for company.

It was during this time that I said "yes" to a trip that would change the course of my life. For it was during this trip that I realised why I'd felt different all my life and why I'd never been able to stay long with all the boys I'd met.

I'll describe one of the scenes that remain vividly with me to this day. We sat next to each other, in silence. She couldn't bear to look at me and, instead, stared out of the window for the entire duration of the six-hour journey up to the mountains. She was aghast at what had happened between us the night before after a few drinks, perhaps more. I can't say I know exactly what she was feeling that day, but I imagine it was at the very least, shame. I, on the other hand, felt nothing of the sort. Yet for me, that journey marked the beginning of a long cycle of utter heartbreak and misery.

'You've always felt that way about me,' she said to me a few days later. Confused by her words, I mentally scanned back over our friendship, which had begun years earlier. Maybe she was right. But if so, I certainly hadn't realised it at the time, and all those years later when it came and hit me so hard, I could hardly breathe. After all the time I had broken other people's hearts, now it was my turn. For the next few years our long-standing friendship struggled on, despite the fact it continually broke my heart while barely denting hers. I kept going back for more in the hope that she might love me as I did her, until eventually one day I was so stressed that I forgot to stop at a roundabout and almost ran over a motorcyclist. It had all become too much. A close friend sent me off to visit a psychic in a little house off Earl's Court Road. I was intrigued, broken and hopeful she could fix me. Once inside, sitting crumpled and defeated on the sofa, I was told in no uncertain terms that I must remove myself from the relationship and cut all ties with my friend in order to mend my broken heart.

Perhaps the most surprising aspect of this story is that it is one of enduring friendship, because while there was a period of time when I didn't want to see her, so that I could regain my sanity, the woman I once loved so much is now a dear friend. I still love her, but in a very different way. And therein lies another lesson from which to carve a guiding principle: Find connection with yourself, always. I had spent so much time looking outside myself that what was really going on inside went unnoticed for so long.

My friend and I have seen and experienced so much together, and I treasure her as one of my closest and dearest companions. She was also my first real love and the key that opened the door to a new and, for a while, secret life. It wasn't so much that I felt gay, more that I didn't really distinguish between sexes. For me and many like me, it's the person that matters, and I'm not comfortable or happy when I hear sexuality being pigeonholed and strictly defined. I don't like putting people in boxes and sticking labels on them. Life is fluid and so are the loves of human beings.

The benefits of being open-minded

Things changed dramatically again for me during my early 30s. I finally found the job of my dreams, having been invited to join a brand-new travel experiences start-up where I could really make a mark and fully embrace my love of all things adventurous, experiential and innovative. So much so that I remained there for almost 13 years. A few years in I was heading the company up as its CEO. I loved the product, I loved the clients and more than anything, I loved the people we employed to work there. We still meet up for adventures together even now, bonded by our love of good food and for the time we shared in a scruffy little office in Battersea.

Alone one night in Balham, my flat mate had gone away for the weekend and it was midnight when I finally plucked up the courage to open *The Times* and leaf through its pages until the one I'd been looking for stared back at me inquisitively. It read, "Lonely Hearts" and I felt a wave of excitement and sheer terror all at once. I scanned through the dozens if not hundreds of "men looking for women" and "women looking for men" adverts before I saw it, in tiny print at the bottom of the page: "Women looking for women." There were just three entries. With all the experience of an utter novice, I read each one carefully and impulsively picked out my choice.

To this day I cannot explain why I called that particular mailbox number, but I did and I listened to the recorded message. A woman's voice, beautifully toned, described her perfect date as ideally Asian, preferably dark-skinned with dark eyes and dark hair. Hmm. I was fair-haired and blue-eyed, but still, what the hell! I shakily left my reply. "Hi, I'm Justine. I'm not quite what you're looking for, but call me anyway." Despite all the close friends I have had, not one of them knew about that period of my life. No one knew about that call.

I nervously waited a few days until a reply came from a dark-haired, dark-eyed woman called Sue. I'd been hoping for a blue-eyed, blonde woman called something like Lauren, and told her so. We laughed at the irony and we talked. In fact, we talked for hours and hours. Then we talked more. For three months. Now, you may well be thinking that is a mighty long, taking-it-slow kind of date, but we had both agreed that we were not what each other was looking for. Yet still, we talked. For my part, our conversations were pure soul food. I'd finally found someone I could be open with about how I'd felt all those years. Someone I could be myself with. I found great comfort and solace in those hours of conversation with a woman who understood my journey, my pain, my shame, my guilt, my heartbreak, my confusion.

Over the course of all those conversations, our friendship

turned to love, and eventually, after many ups and downs, twists and turns, I found my lifelong soul mate in Sue. She was my first real partner and looks like she'll be my last. Despite knowing from those first tentative conversations that we were utterly different, we always find a way to make it work. She gets infuriated by the way I say "yes" to everything without looking into the details. She despairs at how I often have no idea where the road I am taking leads to. But I suspect that underneath it all, that is also what she also loves about me. I like order and tidiness; she is a messy Virgo – what are the chances? And therein lies my next guiding principle: Be open-minded. We are a great example of why it's worth the risk.

Finally meeting someone of the same sex I wanted to settle down with, eventually meant I'd need to tackle the dreaded "coming out" phase of my new life with friends and family. It didn't happen overnight, more like years, and I remember it as a terribly exhausting period. Each time I'd have to summon up the courage to tell another friend at an appropriate time and go through the whole backstory. Time and time again I'd be amazed and incredibly relieved at how supportive they were. Not one of them rejected me, which was an enormous relief. In fact, in 18 years, I don't remember a time when I've experienced any kind of unkindness or discrimination as a result of my sexuality. Sue and I are both careful not to flaunt our relationship in public and some might say we still hide it to some degree. But neither of us sees the point in shouting from the rooftops about it or shoving it in people's faces. Whether that's right or wrong, living honestly or not, I cannot say, but it's the way we are.

It wasn't entirely the same story with my parents. When I first got the courage to give my family the news – at 1am after several glasses of wine – they all hugged me. They accepted it and were okay with it. Then, a week later, it appeared that was not quite the case and after some consideration of a future with no grandchildren – my sister never had children either – my mum called me.

'I can't pretend I'm not disappointed,' she told me in dismay down the phone. It's a conversation that will always remain with me and one I still think about all these years later. I was upset, of course. I could have been angry, sad or intolerant of their feelings, too. But instead, I prefer to be compassionate about a situation they would not have chosen for themselves. I empathise with their feelings and sometimes, when I see a family playing on the beach, I feel a pang of guilt that my parents will never experience the joy of having grandchildren, or seeing their daughter settled with the man of her dreams. There are times when I feel sad that I will never experience being a mother. But whether that's a story of sexuality, or of not having children, doesn't really matter. What matters is that I have been free to make these choices, however difficult. I am grateful for this freedom because so many people around the world are not so free, or so lucky, nor do they have people around them who are, given time in some cases, so accepting.

A deeper look inside

In the past few years, since leaving the travel company I loved so much, I've set up two businesses of my own, one with a foot still in the world of travel and experiences, and the other embracing my new curiosity about wellbeing. In the past 15 years I've tried it all, from kinesiology to breathwork, yoga and Celtic shamanism. I have explored nutrition and the idea that being in nature, particularly forest environments, can play a fundamental part in our wellbeing. As being by or in water has always been so important to me, last year I crowdfunded a little community project to encourage people back into the sea, called the Selsey Sea

Bathing Society. This has been an incredibly rewarding experience and I know there will be so many adventures yet to come.

Last year I began training as a forest bathing – or *shinrin-yoku*, in Japanese – practitioner, teaching people how to reconnect with the natural world. One of the most striking things I've learned is that as a species, we've spent seven to ten million years living within forest environments and only 10,000 years living outside them. No wonder we feel something is missing in our modern world. Yet incredulously, we still can't quite work out what it is, even though it's staring us right in the face.

Alongside all this, over the past decade and a half, I've come to understand that our breath is another missing piece of the puzzle to wholeness. It's an incredible tool to reconnect us to ourselves, to our bodies, for alleviating stress and improving immunity and resilience. And so another, perhaps final, chapter of my career begins. I believe that teaching people about the breath, along with reconnecting to nature through forest bathing, will give people many of the tools they need to navigate the bright new future we so desperately need.

Up until a few years ago, I worried about my approach to life, flitting from one thing to the next, never quite knowing where to lay my hat. I'd always admired people who knew what they wanted to be – a dentist, a lawyer, a doctor. They had a goal and reached out for it. It wasn't until I heard Elizabeth Gilbert, author of *Eat, Pray, Love* and *Big Magic* talk on the subject that I began to feel that perhaps I wasn't such a misfit after all.

Her explanation was that there are two types of people in life. There are jackhammers, which she considered herself to be. These people are efficient and focus on one thing for life. They get the job done but tend to be a bit obsessive and fundamentalist. How I longed to be a jackhammer! But then there are hummingbirds. Moving from tree to tree and flower to flower, hummingbirds make incredibly rich and complex lives for them-selves. They also end up cross-pollinating the world, bringing an idea from one place and taking it to another, mixing things up and being open to new, fresh opportunities that appear.

Listening to her speak, I could not believe what I was hearing. There were actually other people like me! Not only that, but she was also making us sound exciting! All at once I felt more normal and more accepting of myself. All I needed was to trust. And if I did, Elizabeth promised that hummingbirds like me would look up and realise: 'I am exactly where I'm meant to be, with the people I'm meant to be with, in the place that's right for me, right now.'

Can you let go?

We're nearing the end of my story, for now at least. I've just turned 50 and as I write this, I'm saying "yes" to a new round of adventures and opportunities that seem to be presenting them-selves to me and promising a different way of life, yet again.

I'm not sure where you are in your life, but for a moment I wonder if I could invite you to imagine stepping into a maze that represents your own life's journey. You turn right and there's a knowledge that you're on a path that will take you directly to the centre. There, waiting patiently for you is your heart's desire – all your wishes and dreams fulfilled. It feels joyous; you are elated and feel as though you are heading home. Yet a moment later, you take a wrong turn and find yourself back where you began. Those joyous feelings quickly turn to frustration, disappoint-ment and disconnection from what could have been.

Is it fear or stubbornness that stops you from moving forward now? Is that what stops us all? Or are we all just blind to the possibilities of who and what we could be, and what we could make of our lives if we just let go a little more. Are you afraid?

Don't be. Undoubtedly at times, I have filled my life with distractions in order to avoid the fear of connecting to who I really am. Never really feeling too deeply in case I got hurt. Switching on the radio, making a call to a friend, looking at the phone, finding something productive to do. So many of us, I realise, are living our lives on the surface of the ocean, never brave enough to dive beneath; too afraid to feel the joy, the pain, to truly be ourselves, to feel and share the vulnerability deep inside us.

And so, if you realise, after reading this, that you, too, are one of life's hummingbirds, let go of that constant search to find your one true passion, forever feeling disappointed that you haven't found it. Say "yes" instead, to curiosity. Follow it, trust yourself. Let go of the fear and see where it takes you, because it might just take you right to the centre of that maze. To your heart's desire – right where you were meant to be, after all.

Titanium

By Julia Record

Titanium

*"It was serendipity that an ear infection led
to the discovery of my brain tumour.
I was destined to live."*

'Any out-of-body experiences?'

'Oh yes, I've had plenty of them.'

'Are you hearing voices, Julia? Any sudden religious conversions? What about personality changes?'

'No to all of those.'

'Unusual hobbies?'

'Well, I enjoy drinking Earl Grey tea in bed in the morning while reading *House & Garden*. But is that so unusual?'

'What's this?' He held up a pen.

'Well, I don't know what brand it is. It's not Mont Blanc.'

'What about this then?' He pointed to the nib.

It occurred to me then that the answers were quite simply a pen and its nib, and that I had overthought the earlier question. Typical of someone who works in the luxury industry.

By now, I was wondering if I had walked into the right room. Here I was at 78 Harley Street, meeting Mr Bassi for the first time; a man who, though I didn't know it at the time, was going to play an integral part of my life; a man who every year, apart from during the Covid-19 pandemic, I was going to hug, whether it was appropriate or not, such was my bond with him; a man who I would come to hold in the very highest esteem.

'Julia, you have a massive brain tumour and we need to remove it urgently. You've had it for over 20 years and it's pressing heavily on your brain. I'm now sending you to see a neurologist as we need to test some functions, as it's possible that you've had some brain damage.'

I wasn't prepared for such an announcement as I had no symptoms – no headaches, no vision loss, no mobility problems – and yet, I was calm as I walked immediately afterwards to see the next consultant, a specialist in cerebrovascular disease, emergency neurology and movement disorder. Dr Weeks asked me to walk across the room – it was only about five paces. I was bemused. This was truly a surreal experience. What was coming next? And was this itself an out-of-body experience? He then asked me to raise my arms and to follow with my eyes his wavering finger. Dr Weeks said there appeared to be no brain damage. It was hard to believe that, only an hour ago, my life had been following its established routines and patterns.

The next few weeks involved multiple medical checks and more detailed brain scans. I braced myself for the steroids I had to take in preparation for the brain surgery. I assumed I would blow up like Violet Beauregarde from Roald Dahl's *Charlie and the Chocolate Factory*. I was waiting for the mischievous Oompa-Loompas to appear at any moment to tell me it was all a practical joke and my comeuppance was complete.

I had to come to terms with the impending six-to-seven-hour procedure, which would involve three specialist surgeons. I cried just once, but then life became a mission to get everything done in advance of the operation. I reminded myself continually that such a pivot in life is a turning point and not an end point. I was told I would need six months off work. I had guessed that it would be just a few days away from the office, so when told this by the surgeon, I swore uncontrollably in astonishment, as if I had Tourette's syndrome. I had never taken a day off for illness in 30 years of working, except for a stint at the Hospital for Tropical Diseases after a visit to Cameroon's rainforests in my mid-20s.

Apart from the endless medical visits, I had to write my expression of wishes as an adjunct to my will, detailing where I wanted specific belongings to find new homes if the worst were to happen. I had to come to terms with previously unthinkable possibilities. My sister sprang into action, helping me with a Power of Attorney in case the op left me paralysed or brain-dead.

A simple twist of fate

Let me tell you how I ended up at 78 Harley Street, given I had no symptoms apart from the out-of-body experiences, which I had never associated with any physical disorder.

It started with a simple ear infection; an awful one but still just an ear infection. It happened after flying with a cold in the summer of 2014 and led to two weeks of excruciating pain. So much so that, in the middle of one night, I ended up in Accident & Emergency at the local hospital, where I was incorrectly told that I had a perforated eardrum.

My hearing subsequently deteriorated in one ear and I sought the counsel of an ear, nose and throat consultant. The first one I saw told me that my hearing would improve if I took a salt solution and held my nose and swallowed. Six months later, in early 2015, I made an appointment with another specialist, who referred me for an MRI.

I was nervous heading to that fateful MRI as I had suffered a panic attack during a previous one. I told myself that for 15 minutes I could summon the strength through "mind over matter". Two hours later I was still in that tube listening to Frank Sinatra's *My Way*. Not the best song to hear at that time.

The radiologist explained nothing but repeatedly said 'we need to do some more imaging.' I emerged on a Friday night at 8.17pm from a 6pm appointment, only to have to wait until the following Monday for the consultant to deliver my fate.

Cause and effect

More than 11,000 people are diagnosed with a primary brain tumour in the UK each year, of which about half are cancerous. Median life expectancy for glioblastoma, the most common form of primary malignant brain tumour, is only 15 months if one receives surgery, chemotherapy and radiation treatment, but many die much sooner. It's one of life's quickest killers.

The cause of most brain tumours is unknown. My mother blamed my father for carrying me on his shoulders into the hospital at the age of 18 months when my sister was born. He forgot the height of the door. Personally, I wondered if it was due to my exposure to radiation several months after the Chernobyl disaster, while I was living in Romania in my late teens. No one really knows. The geneticist later told me that a genetic malfunction probably took place during my latter stages in the womb, but most brain tumours are not hereditary.

Going back to those out-of-body experiences, I had them frequently as a teenager and into my mid-30s, often when I was in the shower – was it the steamy heat that triggered them? I confided only in my mother about what I termed my 'funny feelings' as I thought no one else would believe me. I knew it was weird. I assumed they may have been a result of my being quite spiritual.

Though I never met my paternal grandmother – she had died four years before I was born, having been treated incorrectly for a mental disorder with electric shock treatment – by all accounts Maud Charlotte had been a spiritual woman. She used to see a monk at the end of her bed and had the most extraordinary gift of intuition. Some people say that psychic gifts skip a generation and I had rather hoped her skills had been passed to me and my out-of-body experiences were a gift from her.

Mr Bassi explained that the reason he asked me about whether I had such experiences was that they could be a sign of a growing brain tumour. Naturally, I was deeply disappointed that my out-of-body episodes could be explained by a physical malfunction and that I wasn't very special after all.

Banishing negative energy

While preparing for my brain surgery, I was also trying to expel a negative force from the Regency house that I had recently bought and restored. The house's energy just didn't feel quite right and I wondered if it was due to my determined builder having thrown in the skip what he suggested may have been human bones that had been discovered when digging out the vaults.

My street had been heavily bombed in the Second World War and was situated in one of Westminster's most historical areas, near a plague pit called Tothill Fields – now Vincent Square. I was horrified that these bones had been discarded in such a blasé way, with no ritual or ceremony to honour the dead and without discussion. But the builder said it had been necessary as otherwise the building site could have been immediately closed down by the local council.

To restore the right kind of energy to my house, I had been searching for some holy water. One evening while out walking in the lead-up to my surgery, I came across the lit-up St Stephen's Church in Westminster's Rochester Row. St Stephen's was built by Angela Burdett-Coutts (1814-1906), granddaughter and heiress of the banker, Thomas Coutts. She intended it as a memorial to her father, Sir Francis Burdett, a brilliant and radical former MP for Westminster. With the encouragement of her close friend and author, Charles Dickens, she chose to build it in a very poor area on the edge of the notorious Devil's Acre, on land donated by the Dean and Chapter of Westminster Abbey.

As I walked into the church I was given a hymn book. I returned it immediately and explained that I wasn't there for the service but instead to receive some holy water I could take with me for my possibly haunted home. I then had second thoughts about the church service and wondered if it was serendipity that I had arrived as evensong got under way.

I was the last person to leave following the service and I couldn't help but blurt out to the vicar, as he stood at the door bidding his farewells, that I had recently moved into a house that had a strange, indescribable sense. Not only did he offer to visit with the holy water for which I had been on a quest, but he also said he would conduct a ceremony to bless the house.

'I've just been diagnosed with a giant brain tumour,' I interjected, 'is there anything you can do for that while you're at it?' The Reverend peered at me quizzically. This wasn't his usual end-of-service conversation. A week later, as he performed the blessing and ushered out the evil spirits, he seemed similarly taken aback when the gas flames in my house quavered in a highly unusual pattern.

Then I can't remember how, but it was suddenly the day before my brain surgery and I took the day off to revisit St Stephen's, where I was jolted into a new awareness of the spiritual, the physical, and their indivisibility. The vicar blessed me by laying hands on my head. I thought again of the remarkable story of Angela Burdett-Coutts, who had financed the church, and what a rebellious life she led despite Victorian restraint.

When she was 67, she shocked polite society by marrying her 29-year-old secretary, who became MP for Westminster in 1881. Her husband had been born in America, so a clause in her step-grandmother's will forbidding her heir to marry a foreign national was invoked and Burdett-Coutts forfeited three-fifths of her income. She nonetheless chose to spend the majority of her wealth as a pioneer in social housing, which led Queen Victoria to make her the first female peer. I digress, but I love the story of an independent woman with a purpose – it was an inspirational tale to position my mind in a frame of fortitude and stoicism for what was to come.

After the laying on of hands at church, it was off to the hairdresser in the final hours of the eve of my surgery. I had worn my hair long since I was four, but in preparation for the shaving of my head I thought it was practical to cut it short. I felt like I was preparing to be beheaded. A tear rolled down my cheek at the sight of the dramatic change to my appearance, to which I had been accustomed for many decades.

At about 7pm I went to the office to prepare and submit my expenses, knowing that I would be away recovering for six months. I hate and continually delay doing expenses, and I couldn't believe that I was spending potentially the last hours of my life doing something so routine and unimportant.

These details illustrate how I was so busy before the surgery that I really didn't dwell too much on what was about to happen. Perhaps that was a good thing? It certainly was a positive step not to have Googled "brain tumours" in advance, as I still had little idea of how serious my condition was.

I arrived home at about 9.30pm to finalise my Power of Attorney and last wishes. Now that was indeed a miserable and depressing thing to do on a dark winter's night before part of my skull was to be removed.

The reality of risk

The following morning as my then-partner Mark prepared to drive me to the Harley Street clinic, each scrape of the squeegee across the frosted windscreen felt like a moment of reprieve. But we got there, of course. They gave me the best suite in the hospital. I work in hotels and finally I had received an upgrade of my own. Two windows instead of one, a small triumph in advance of my life-saving surgery.

The surgeons arrived to prepare me for six hours in the operating theatre. I said I hoped they hadn't been together the night before, drinking copiously. They shared a look and a spark of levity for me became a flame of worry. What if human frailty and error converged to result in my paralysis, brain damage or death? The result of their work was not in my control and I realised that I wasn't prepared for what was coming next.

I had been busy with work and the principal surgeon, Mr Bassi, had only briefly explained the risks of the procedure the first time we had met in his plush consulting rooms. Now he went into extraordinary detail about what could go wrong in the operating room. I knew this was standard procedure, but I had not stopped to consider seriously that these might be my last thoughts. I started shaking uncontrollably for what seemed like an eternity. The nurse asked if I was ready to be 'brought down.' I felt like I was on death row.

At times like this the body goes into automatic "fight or flight" mode. I was actually considering going on the run. Then reason took over – if I ran away I would slowly become brain damaged and start losing my sight, language ability and mobility. The idea of choice was an illusion. Normally I would have hugged my partner before being 'brought down' but I knew that if I did that I would break down uncontrollably, further delaying the inevitable. No, I was going to keep myself under control and get on with what had to happen if I was to fight for the rest of my life. No eye contact. No emotion.

The anaesthetist was South African. As he began to work I asked if he knew my old boss, the South African visionary hotelier Sol Kerzner. He was a close friend, which was a weirdly reassuring connection at a time of unfamiliarity. I asked the operating nurse to hold my hand while the cold anaesthetic ran through my veins. I was aware that there would be something paradoxical and unsettling about my personal absence during the most vital few hours of my life.

A strange awakening

When I awoke from the anaesthetic I saw the neurosurgeons peering down at me, repeating my name. I became aware that I was being wheeled from the recovery room on a trolley into critical care. Here I would remain with at least one permanent carer and multiple wires plugged into numerous machines for the next 48 hours or so before moving to my upgraded hospital room.

Next, Mr Bassi was tickling my feet: could I feel the sensation? Euphoria. I wasn't paralysed. I could feel his touch, but also an unfamiliar feeling between my legs. A catheter. No one had told me about this in advance and I hadn't even thought about how I would pee. But it was irrelevant. I was alive. I was a survivor.

My sister arrived and held my hand. I even managed to say a few words: I told her that I loved her and she said she loved me. That is the only time we have said that to each other.

The day after the brain tumour was removed, Mr Bassi warned me that my eyes would close over from the heavy bruising to my brain. I would look like I had 'undergone several rounds with Mike Tyson.' Sure enough, my eyes began to close. It was actually a relief as I felt unable to look in the bathroom mirror, which I had requested to be covered knowing that my head was partially shaven, I would possess a new dent in my right temple and a 25cm-long, 39-stitch scar shaped like a question mark.

Then the hallucinations started.

I connected with the soul of a lion through his eyes. Locking eyes with such a majestic animal despite my temporary blindness was mesmerising. I was in a magical land – it was Narnia and I was with Aslan. Engulfed in a field of protection, I saw the gentleness of a killer. The King of the Jungle is the ultimate symbol of overcoming challenges. I wasn't aware of 'spirit animals' at the time, but several years later I discovered that, if the lion appears to you, its presence as a spirit guide can be symbolic of unrivalled courage and the power to push through life, no matter what.

The lion totem often comes into your life when you are facing a moment of weakness, to strengthen and embolden you. It urges you to move forward with intrepidness and decisiveness. I've now become fascinated by spirit guides and every time I see a lion, whether a statue or in the flesh, it brings me back to that seismic recovery time when I truly understood the power of life.

My sense that I was playing an unwanted leading role in a film was made even more dramatic by the soundtrack that was playing. I could hear a constant drum beat. As my eyes were closed from the bruising, at first I assumed that the nurses had left the television or radio on. I kept asking them to turn off the sound but they told me there was nothing to turn off.

Finally, it dawned on me that perhaps the neurosurgeons had been playing music during the operation and maybe I hadn't been as entirely absent under anaesthetic as I thought. I imagined it must have been the kind of Hollywood blockbuster music that plays when the heroine emerges triumphant and resilient from a bad love affair. Mr Bassi informed me that it had, in fact, been hits by Guns N' Roses and Happy Mondays. After two weeks the music in my head stopped.

Insight and understanding

The surgery took place on February 27, 2015: a date entrenched in my memory for evermore. Two days later, Mr Bassi gave me mixed news: the tumour had come out in full and was, thankfully, benign; however, they unexpectedly found another brain tumour at the subsequent MRI, this time on my right temporal lobe. This tumour was small and also looked benign but needed annual monitoring and, perhaps, future surgery if it grew.

It was total good fortune that my initial ear infection led to the discovery of an unrelated brain tumour. I was destined to live. Now my search is for the purpose of this gift of life. My intuition tells me it might be about bringing together communities through private enterprise. I have become involved in a wonderful charity called Debate Mate, which powers social change through debating, building confidence and critical thinking from the classroom to the boardroom. "Win with your heart, and then your skills" could be their mantra.

I agree wholeheartedly with American author and presidential speechwriter James Humes when he said: 'The art of communication is the language of leadership.' With social media and artificial intelligence taking increasing hold, the truly differentiating skill set of the future will be charismatic communication that combines intelligence, insight, understanding and wisdom.

"Intelligence tells you what to do. Insight tells you how to do it. Understanding tells you when to do it. Wisdom tells you why you do it," summed up the philosopher Matshona Dhliwayo.

While researching for this chapter I found an email from my then-partner to my friends. I was struck by this excerpt:

'The best news is that the results of the biopsy of the tumour have confirmed that it was benign.

'Mr Bassi said that it had been there for more than 20 years, and it was serendipitous that it was found, by chance, when it was, because in his opinion, Julia would have begun to show symptoms in a matter of months. This would have been due to the existing pressure of the tumour increasing on the brain, which would have started to cause actual brain damage.

'We can only thank God that it was found when it was and Julia is so grateful that she has been given a second chance.'

Indeed, I know I have a chance to be curious and fearless; to appreciate the value of the moment and not wait until it becomes a memory; to know that how we deal with disappointment will be the measure of our success; to create the habit of persistence to make it the habit of victory; to change what we can control, accept what we cannot and to know the difference. I'm also reminded that 'the nobility of a being is measured by its capacity for gratitude' (The Mother).

I will always be grateful to Mark for being in my life at the right time, and I have him to thank for my love of the song *Titanium* by David Guetta, in honour of the titanium plates now holding my skull together. Nothing beats dancing to that song in my kitchen to lift my spirits. Life may not be the party we hoped for, but while we are here, we might as well dance.

'I'm bulletproof, nothing to lose / Fire away, fire away
Ricochet, you take your aim / Fire away, fire away
You shoot me down, but I won't fall / I am titanium
You shoot me down, but I won't fall / I am titanium'

I'm not invincible. I'm human: complex, vulnerable and fearful. Confucius said a man has two lives and that the second life begins when he realises he only has one. Mortal I am, but titanium I remain; a believer in second chances.

Trust That Whisper in Your Heart

By Sharan Patel

Trust That Whisper
in Your Heart

*"My rebellion was fuelled by having to fight for
the opportunities that were easily available
to the men in my family."*

A person's greatest treasure is the wisdom in his or her own heart, no matter how old or young. Trust that inner whisper.

We are born with great treasures and wisdom etched in our hearts and minds, and every now and then this wisdom whispers or shouts. We go through various phases of our lives and are influenced by our families, our teachers and the people who cross our paths. There could also be political upheavals that change our environments and influence our perception of life, no matter our age.

I was born into a loving family to much older parents in Kenya, in a small town called Elburgon, which was surrounded by deep jungle. On that day, my great aunt, who lived with us, said she heard a lion roar nearby, and that I roared too.

I had a very liberal Indian upbringing in a spiritual and religiously tolerant environment with strong values placed on education and having good *sanskar*. In a broad sense, this translates as principles or standards of ethical behaviour, deep-rooted values and virtues.

I had a great education. At the age of 11, I went to a convent school in a place called Eldoret. On our first day, the Mother Superior said that, as a woman, she had chosen a path to serve God, and we could do anything we wanted in the world. At that time we didn't actually understand what she meant.

Throughout my childhood, I questioned strong views on following conventions. One of the big ones for me was around marriage. When I was 11, my parents went to India and brought back my wedding saris. I remember looking at the saris and knowing that I would never wear them. What was within me, at the age of 11, that whispered to me that I needed/wanted to do more than follow tradition and convention?

My great aunt was a real influence on me and her endearing words guided me to trust what is so strong in my heart. She also said she knew that somewhere deep within me, I had the strength of a lion. I didn't understand what that meant until much later.

I knew from a very young age that I wanted to experience more than what was in front of and around me. I could see so much unfairness and I wanted to make a difference. I questioned and rebelled at what I felt wasn't fair. I remember hearing about the suicide of a family friend who was a young, beautiful lady. She had fallen in love with a man she met at school and yet her family was forcing her to marry someone they had chosen. How unfair was this? She must have been so distraught and lost the will to live.

Of course, some of my rebellion was dismissed by the adults as growing out of the typical challenges of youth. I rebelled against the tradition to marry only that person who was approved by my family and the society I lived in. My rebellion was also fuelled by having to fight for the opportunities that were easily available to the men in my family, especially when they didn't take them. Yet I knew that I was correct and this created so much angst for me. I felt I was letting the family down. The little girl in me sought approval and recognition. I was too young to understand then that if I simply trusted my heart, I would remain detached and not so worried about the outcome. Belief in myself and my life would have been so much easier. I had to learn the lessons along the way to be who I am now, and boy did I learn them!

A time of destiny

The Hindu Holy Scriptures, *Bhagavad Gita*, state that our soul chooses to be born in the family we are in. Our soul will journey with the family and accept the journey. In the Hindu tradition a child's name-giving ceremony is performed on the sixth day after its birth – in Sanskrit it is called *chhathi na lekh*. According to folklore, there was a belief that on this day, Vidhaata, the god of destiny, would quietly enter the house around midnight to pen the destiny of the newborn.

On the eve of the sixth day after the birth, the baby is dressed in new clothes. The mother holds the baby near the *gadi* or *mandir*, the altar, where photos or statues of gods and goddesses are placed. One lights a lamp known as a *diya* with a wick soaked in ghee, which is purified butter. Blank pieces of paper and a red pen are placed on a *baajhat*, a wooden plank, for Vidhaata to write the future of the newborn. Clean white handkerchiefs and extra pens are also placed there so that after they have been blessed they can be used on future auspicious occasions. Some families also soak *kumkum*, a red powder, with water to stamp the baby's footprints on blank paper or cloth. This is to guide Vidhaata to the baby. Later it can be used as a keepsake.

Some may see this as a superstition. Traditions and rituals in all cultures are a matter of faith and they exist as guidance. It is not to say that if you don't perform these rituals, your baby will not enjoy a good future.

I was told that when this ceremony was done for me, I kept moving my feet, as if trying to walk. My great aunt said to me years later that it had looked as if I were simply going to keep moving and moving. Of course, I didn't realise the significance of it all until just recently, as I have indeed walked away from many things; conventions, difficult relationships, countries and much more.

My great aunt, in her quiet way, taught me that I should challenge conventions and that everyone I would meet in life would have a message for growth. She was a very beautiful woman with an amazing soul, and such a guiding spirit. She was a great cook and had so much patience. I loved being with her and she always consoled me when I was upset. When I was young I was very curious about her, but there seemed to be something of a mystery around her. There were conversations in hushed tones, which I didn't understand.

We could not discuss anything about the unfairness of the way the Muslims were treating the Hindus in Pakistan. Also, when Pakistan went to war with India over Kashmir, our family decided that there would be no access to the radio or television, so that we could not hear any news.

When I was older, I learnt that my aunt was born in the part of India that became Pakistan, and she followed the Islamic faith. She defied convention and married my great uncle, who was Hindu, and they lived in the province of Sindh. My great uncle was banished from the family. In 1947, when India earned independence from the British and Pakistan was created, Sindh became part of Pakistan. All Hindus had to either convert to Islam or leave Pakistan. My great uncle died during this civil unrest and my grandfather managed to bring my great aunt to India to live with them. As my parents were in Kenya, it was agreed that she would come and live with us. I am so glad she did. I believe that she did follow both faiths: Islam and Hinduism. Oh, how I wish she was still alive and I could ask her so many questions. I learnt a lot from her and I feel her soul still with me.

A move to the Big Apple

I completed my studies in England before returning to Kenya to work with the United Nations Development Program. The pressures to marry were huge. I was introduced to nice young men from prominent families and there was always a singular push toward getting married. I decided to escape that pressure from my family, that shoves toward convention, and eventually ended up in New York.

In the queue at the US embassy while getting my visas to go to New York, I met a magical man with a beautiful name, Lloyd Archibald-Williams. He happened to be a recruitment consultant, and when I fell in love with New York, Lloyd helped me to find an amazing job there. I worked in New York for ten years and have often given thanks for the blessing of fortuitously meeting Lloyd.

A school friend of mine named Richard was living in Chicago and then moved to New York. We started dating and after a year decided to buy an apartment in a converted brownstone. I was in my element. I was living in a vibrant city, enjoyed my work, though it was challenging, and was a co-owner of my first home. I bought my first piece of China and enjoyed making the apartment cosy and comfortable. We worked hard and played hard; I trained for the New York Marathon and met amazing people, and we had exciting impromptu parties.

Richard's younger brother, Sam, was visiting us one summer

and the two of us were watching a film called *Where Eagles Dare*. Toward the end there is a captivating scene on a cable car – it really puts you on the edge of your seat. Richard was setting up a new music system in the living room – his new toy, he loved gadgets – and called to us in to see it. I said that we would join him as soon as the film was over, but a few minutes later he came into the room and just switched off the television. Both Sam and I had been so engrossed and we became annoyed with him. Though I very rarely swear, I told him to f**k off and I switched the TV back on. I must admit I was shocked at myself, and Richard, aghast, looked at me defiantly. He then lifted his hand and hit me hard across the face. No one had ever hit me. I couldn't believe what had just happened.

Sam yelled at his brother and apologised to me. I can't think of words to describe how I felt: shock, puzzlement, anger? To this day I don't have one word to describe that moment. I looked at Richard and in my best imitation of a calm voice, simply said 'That's it. I am leaving.' I started packing some clothes. Sam was crying and begged me not to go. Richard snatched my bag and said that he wouldn't let me go. I looked at him and told him I was not waiting for him to hit me again. I just knew that if he had done it once, he would do it again. I left my apartment with whatever I could grab and I stood on 88th Street in the middle of Manhattan, alone, with no home and no family to go to. Despite all that, I knew that I had made the right decision.

A good friend's cousin had been a founding member of the Southall Black Sisters, which was set up in 1979 to defend the human rights of Asian women who are victims of domestic violence. She reached out to family members to volunteer, and a few times had asked me to help her by taking some women, who had been victims of domestic violence, to a safe house.

I didn't even know the names of these women, but I could see the scars and bruises on them. They talked to me while I drove. Oh, how my heart went out to them. During the few months that I volunteered, I noticed that sometimes I drove the same women to safety. I realised that they would often go back to their husbands, as they could not face life on their own. They were so vulnerable.

I knew deep inside me that if ever a man hit me, I would not wait for more. And it was that strong internal voice that gave me the courage to walk out of my apartment that day. Richard begged for forgiveness and promised he would never hit me again, but the memory of those women in the back of my car gave me courage. I wasn't willing to chance it.

From learning to teaching

It was two years before I could finally move on financially from Richard. I couldn't tell my family about this situation. They thought that, once again, I was moving away from a 'suitable boy.'

I have since learnt that Richard's father used to hit his mother, which made sense of his brother's distress when he saw what he did all those years ago. I reconnected with Richard a few years ago and he asked me if I forgave him. I asked him if he could forgive himself. He had no answer. I told him I had no regrets about my decision.

Once again, I had been reminded of my great aunt's philosophy that every event teaches us a lesson and our wisdom is enriched through the experience.

I left New York and moved back to London, as I wanted to be closer to my family. I could also visit my mother in Kenya more easily from there. I continued to work hard and I did very well in my career. I worked in the Far East, Canada and Europe. There were challenging times at work, and in 2007 I managed to get a two-month sabbatical and took an opportunity to volunteer in Darjeeling, north-east India. I taught in a municipal school where children who attended were provided with a hot lunch. It was heart-breaking to see how many children took food home with them for their family.

I also went to a children's home run by a Buddhist monk, Pema Bhante. There I met two girls who had been rescued from human trafficking. I call them my "angels." Traffickers are conniving and evil, and they would tell parents that their girls would be educated and have opportunities to earn a lot of money. Once rescued, the girls cannot be returned home, as the parents would sell them again.

The unfairness of the two girls' situation deeply affected me. I took on a project to educate them and now they have their own small business. But I wanted to do even more, so I founded the Darjeeling Children's Trust with a group of amazing people who came into my life while volunteering. We have raised more than £800,000 and have helped many children. We are now rebuilding the children's home and, at the time of writing, we are finalists for the Charity of the Year Award from the British Indian Association.

The children I meet in Darjeeling teach me so much. They have very little or nothing and yet they are happy. They smile eternally and sing with joy at the simplest gift. This has been, by far, my most rewarding work. I was recently told that I am like a lioness when it comes to these children. I do everything to protect them and make sure that they are safe and well. So now I realise that the lion must have roared for a reason when I was born.

I now know that any woman who takes up a cause to fight for goodness and justice is said to have the spirit of the goddess Durga. She is a goddess of war, the warrior form of Parvati, who is Lord Shiva's consort. Her mythology centres around combating evils and demonic forces that threaten peace, prosperity, and *dharma*, the power of good over evil. Durga is also a fierce form of the protective mother goddess, who unleashes her divine wrath against the wicked to liberate the oppressed, and calls on destruction to empower creation. That is how I feel about my children in Darjeeling. We are where we are meant to be and will stay there until we learn our lessons.

A fortuitous meeting

Seeking validation and approval has been a big part of my life since I went out into a world away from conventional family and life. There were times when I wanted to run back to the bosom of my family and be comforted, but as time has gone by, I have learnt to believe in myself, shine my light brightly and speak from my heart with deepest honesty. I may hurt someone, but I must be loving and kind. I am learning that authenticity liberates me and gives me freedom. Though I still have much to learn.

Every person we meet is a gift to us. This is so true of all the people I have met. I have met some who show me what not to do, and others who enable my light to shine.

One day I was sitting on the steps of a building near Cadogan Hall in Sloane Square, London, waiting for the doors to open to hear a lecture on the principles of the Vedanta, a part of old Hindu philosophy. A lady walked past, looking slightly lost. Her name was Fif.

'I'm looking for Cadogan Hall,' she told me.

'I'm waiting for the doors to open as well,' I replied.

'May I sit with you?' Fif asked.

As we conversed, she told me that she was visiting a friend in London on her way to Vancouver, but that she lived in Auroville.

'Auroville! A childhood friend of mine, Nick, lived in Auroville," I told her. "It's a sad story, though; he extended an invitation to me to visit him several times and I planned to visit him one day, but he had suffered a broken leg in a motorbike accident, was admitted to the hospital, caught an infection and died. He was such a great friend and I was so distraught at this great loss.'

Fif looked at me. 'Nick was my good, good friend,' she said. 'We knew each other for many years. I organised Nick's funeral. I was just with his mum the other day.'

'And I was with his mum yesterday," I gasped.

I had goose bumps, but that was not the end of the surprise. The friend who Fif was visiting in London was our dear Claudia Roth, who has been instrumental in gathering together all the stories in this book.

I believe that Nick sent both Fif and Claudia to me. I couldn't get to Auroville, so he made sure Auroville came to me.

The origins of a story

Claudia and all the lovely people I have met through this group of writers have most certainly changed my life. What a gift they have been. Telling my story has removed a weight from me. I have been able to pour my heart out, emptying it of the pain I have felt for so many years. I have shared my experiences with the most supportive group of enlightened women I have ever met, even though most of them I have only met in the virtual world due to the Covid-19 lockdown. But love and support have no barriers. I have learnt that the person one admires is a reflection of one's soul. The quality you see in others is within you. We can each fix the other's crown. Have belief and trust, and shine.

The Power of Pain

By Karin Mlaker

The Power of Pain

"It feels like a wake-up call: I have to do something differently. But what?"

It is Friday evening. I am exhausted. It has been another of those weeks that have characterised my life for the past few years: working in global communications, there are always too many tasks, too many people wanting something, too many meetings and not enough time to think, work or even breathe. On top of this, the daily commute by train is enriched with a bouquet of cruelties: signal failures, broken air conditioning, overcrowding. Here I stand on platform one, and I can't wait for the train to take me home to my nest, where my bed is waiting for me, which I do not intend to leave for the entire weekend.

But I need to be patient. A croaking voice is announcing a delay of 20 minutes that feels like two hours. I want to get away from this place, from the burden. My pulse starts racing again when I think of all my unresolved work tasks, not knowing how to complete them in time and to the quality that is demanded. My boss never tires of repeating that he expects more for the money I earn. He could hire three junior people for what I cost him, and he expects me to work as hard as that imaginary trio, but much faster and better due to my experience. At the same time, he does not allow me to work in my own way. Instead, he puts me in a tight corset of rules and behaviours. My freedom-loving soul is smothered. I am so tired.

Finally, the train arrives. I stand at the edge of the platform watching the lights coming closer and there it is, all of a sudden, the thought that if I just took one step forward I would finally have my peace.

Flashback: 1963-69 I grew up in a place where other people spend their vacations, a place of calm and relaxation. Our little village in Austria, close to the Italian border and surrounded by mountains and lakes, was shaped by the typical serenity of the locals. I had a very happy childhood there, spending most of my time outside with friends. My parents kept an eye on me and my younger brother but also gave us a lot of freedom to expand, have our own experiences and discover the unknown. If we got lost on one of our excursions, somebody from the village would come across us and take us home. I think this way of growing up laid the foundation for me to become the libertine I am today. And who knows how else it would have influenced me had my time there not come to a sudden end in the summer of '69.

I do not step forward. By no means do I want to end my life. I love life! And when there is a problem, I look for a solution and try to solve it in a constructive way. That's what makes this devastating thought from out of the blue even more scary. So scary that I don't trust myself anymore and quickly step back from the edge of the platform to wait until the train comes to a stop. I tremble. My heart is beating even faster, but this time not because of my work. This time it is my own thoughts that provoke me. It feels like a wake-up call: I cannot continue like this. I have to stop. I have to do something differently. But what?

And who can help me with this? I have known for a while that I need to change something. I have spoken several times already with my boss about it. I have made suggestions about how to bring some release into my life and at the same time ensure that the job gets done. But he is always deaf to my ideas. He is not the person to help me find a solution. I decide to see my doctor the next morning, to talk openly about the situation. I hate to do this, as I do not want to admit that I am overwhelmed. I am not familiar with this feeling, so I have not learned how to deal with it. Suddenly I feel so grateful that until now I have been surrounded by people who care about me and who want the best for me. I have taken this psychological safety for granted. Until now. As I sit in this train carriage I realise that I can no longer avoid making some drastic decisions.

Flashback: 1969-70 'We needed to unwind. I guess nothin' can last forever. Forever, no.' This was not only true for Bryan Adams but also for me, back in the summer of '69. Within a couple of weeks, I found myself in a new environment, 800km to the north of my home village. No more mountains as I knew them, no more lakes. No more friends. People still spoke German there, but with a very strange accent. My father, a chemist with ambition, had decided to escape the province and ascend the career ladder. My mother, a housewife, bravely supported him. My brother and I were not asked.

It was a tough start to my new life in Germany. Two weeks after we arrived at our new home I began my first year at school. There I was, the girl from Carinthia, who nobody understood because of her strong Austrian dialect. Everybody had big smiles on their faces and school cones filled with sweets and little presents in their hands. Every pupil received one on their first day to make the start of school seem more inviting. Everybody, that is, except me, as my mother did not know the custom of bringing a school cone. So, everybody could clearly see that I was different before I even opened my mouth. That was the day I learned what it means to be a foreigner.

Surprisingly, when I look back on this dramatic stage of my young life, I do not remember any bad feelings. I guess that's because discovering new places was not new to me. The combination of protection and freedom that I had always known helped me see this move more like a big adventure than a threat. Equipped with this psychological security, I saw it as a great opportunity to learn how to quickly integrate into an unknown environment, to appreciate and adapt to local habits, and to respect individuality. At the age of six, it seems I established a foundation from which to deal with so many new starts that would to come in my life, in Germany, Europe and Asia.

For my doctor, the diagnosis is crystal clear, and she agrees that I urgently need to change something. It is not yet too late, but if I do not react quickly, she fears that I may need to step completely out of my life for a few months to recover. I definitely want to avoid a burnout. I promise her that I will talk to my boss again. She is not very optimistic, as in her experience bosses don't tend to be supportive in such circumstances. She says that as my manager, my boss has a responsibility to care for my wellbeing, and a diagnosis like this reflects badly on him. I am surprised, as I am deeply convinced that everyone should be responsible for their own personal wellbeing. She finally writes my diagnosis and wishes me luck.

The next day, I knock at my manager's door. I am nervous. Now is the moment when I have to admit that I have reached my limits, that I am unable to meet his expectations and I need help to get out of this situation. How will he react? Will this confession open his heart? Or will he try to protect himself?

Flashback: 1970-1982 The company my father had joined went bankrupt, so we moved again after just one year – another 300km further north and just in time to start my second year at school. This time it was a bit easier. Nobody had a school cone and my accent had flattened a bit, but once again I was the new one, the one who was not from here, the one who used funny words, the one who was interesting. I guess this was when I learned that every situation can be seen from at least two different perspectives: strange/interesting, different/unique, new classmates/new chance to make friends, new environment/new discoveries.

Many years later, I learned that this technique is called "reframing" and is a powerful coaching tool as it widens one's perspective when looking at certain situations, people or relationships. Reframing allows me a choice of how to rate whatever happens to me. I can decide whether to be a victim or a designer of my life. I am not sure if it was due to this subconscious ability to take responsibility for my life, or my engaging personality, or the open-minded character of the people around me – maybe it was my mother's divine apple strudel – maybe a little bit of everything, but the fact is that my family and I quickly became part of the community and stayed for 13 years. Until we moved again, all in different directions.

My voice falters and my hand shakes as I give my boss the doctor's diagnosis. I look into his eyes and I am sure that I know how he will react. However, I am wrong. It is even worse than I thought. He doubts that I have too much work to do. He wants me to prove this to him. He does not allow me to work from home on the days my doctor has prescribed treatment for me. His heart is more closed than ever. I am deeply disappointed. How can he be so unemotional? We have worked closely together for many years. I have always been loyal to him and the good feedback that I often receive from senior management also makes him look good. I feel like a cleaning rag that is tossed aside. Nevertheless, I do what he asks. I prove that meetings already take up two-thirds of my normal work time, that every week I put in 60-70 hours and that is still not enough to get things done. He does not trust my calculation. Instead, he reproaches me in front of others for not getting involved enough. I do not have the strength to defend myself. I feel as though I am in the role of the tragic hero in a play that I never auditioned for. Has such a character ever survived until the final curtain? I speak with my doctor about it and she writes me a sick note. The hero exits the stage – for four weeks.

I have never been sick for such a long time. I do not feel comfortable with it but I do not have a choice. I inform my boss and call my main contacts. A colleague tells me that she is not surprised. Everybody has witnessed what has happened to me and most were wondering how long I would be able to cope with it. I learn that some colleagues have even spoken to my boss about it, but he refused to listen. He needs somebody to get the work done and I have always been very reliable and productive.

I begin to question myself. Why did I not talk earlier about my situation to some trusted colleagues? I wish I knew. When in my life did I internalise that I have to be strong and I am not allowed to fail? It is not a message I received from my parents. Maybe it is a consequence of my integration efforts as a child? The "new one" is not allowed to show weakness or others may take advantage. It is a pity that I blocked myself, because it is interesting to find out what others think. My colleague shares an example with me: "Even the best high-jumper cannot jump over a bar that is too high for a human being to reach. You already jumped over a bar that is higher than most of us would have been able to reach."

This makes me suddenly remember the lesson I learnt in childhood; to see every situation from at least two perspectives: Am I not good enough or better than all others? I still have no answer to why I did not speak earlier to a colleague about my situation. But at least I know now that I did not fail. I feel relieved but at this very moment I do not know where this time off will lead me. It feels like the right thing to do though, and I have no doubt anymore that it will guide me in the right direction.

Flashback: 1982-85 After I finished school, I studied tourism management in Austria. Not that I wanted to work there afterwards. I had just one goal and that was to become an air hostess and see the world. Now that I was an experienced "foreigner", I wanted to discover more foreign places and I could see no better way to do this than working for a renowned airline.

It was my father who advised me that I should first finish some studies so I would have a solid basis for the time after my career as an air hostess. I followed his advice and two years later I was ready to apply to Lufthansa. I had no doubt that I would get the job: I had a degree in tourism management, lived in Paris to improve my language skills, was passionate about the work, young enough, tall enough, good-looking enough. When can I start?

Things never took off with Lufthansa, at least not as an air hostess. For whatever reason, my application was rejected. I fell into a deep despair. I had lost my dream, all I desired, and I didn't have an alternative plan. I had to return to my parents, who had moved again and had not expected me to be living with them. This was the last time in my life I would focus on a single goal. I decided to let it flow and instead see what life had to offer me. Of course, I always had some ideas of how I wanted to live and what I would ideally like and not like to do, but more as a suggestion than a plan. By starting to put my trust in life, a career unfolded that I never would have been able to imagine for myself. So, thank you Lufthansa.

Four weeks of taking care of myself is balm for my body and soul. I know that returning to work will not be easy but I am still convinced the break was the right decision. I am nervous. How will my boss react? Once again, the answer is worse than expected. I am demoted, my salary is frozen and I am not allowed to work for senior management anymore. Friends and colleagues ask me, 'Why do you not just quit? You will easily find a new job somewhere else.'

But I do not want to quit because the company is a good fit for me. In more than 20 years in the business, thanks to my diverse network, I have worked for many companies. Most of them I only stayed with for five years before life offered a new, exciting experience in a new and exciting place. Now I have reached a stage where I would love to be settled but without having to stand still.

This is why I am convinced I am working for the right company. There are opportunities for me, I have wonderful colleagues, I am well connected and very well respected. Many colleagues seek my help. I just have the wrong boss. Is there really only an either/or option for me? What do I need to do to continue working for the company without being exploited and humiliated by this man? There must be an "as well as" solution.

Finding a good answer is overwhelming me. I speak with friends and colleagues about it, join courses and read books. I collect many good ideas, evaluate them, let them resonate with me, put them back into the ideas basket. It is obviously a journey. Every idea I receive, every aspect I consider, every technique I learn lays the ground for this journey. And then I find the information I need to be able to decide.

Flashback: 1986-present I jumped in at the deep end and my reward was to work with charismatic entrepreneurs and interna-

tional companies. I witnessed the rapid rise and fall of the dot-com era and travelled around the world – with Lufthansa, but as a customer – working in interesting cities and countries from Brussels to London, Singapore and Chengdu. I learned that I could achieve much more than I ever dreamed of. I just needed to take this little step and say to myself, 'Yes, I will give it a try.' What is the worst that can happen? I either will fail and learn along the way, or I will succeed and learn along the way. In my successes, I would have good reason to share a bottle of Champagne with my companions.

A great success factor was my network, without which there would definitely have been fewer opportunities to say 'yes' to. To be honest, I have never received a single job by just applying for it. I have been the marketing assistant at a British hotel chain, the personal assistant of a German real estate guru, the communications manager for a US telecommunications company and the marketing and communications director for a consulting firm – and I got every single job because somebody had recommended me. These were people I knew from various networks such as the Junior Chamber International, the American Business Association or the Toastmasters. They were also former colleagues with whom I stayed in contact or ex-bosses with whom I had become friends.

It helped a lot that I loved going out and meeting for drinks, as these networks had to be built and maintained without social media. Today, there are much easier – and maybe also healthier – ways to connect. LinkedIn has become a valuable way to keep in touch with people, even when they are far away on the other side of the world. Working Out Loud, a global grassroots movement started by John Stepper in New York, helps build relationships between people, even strangers, who then help each other to reach specific personal goals. These are just two of many networking groups we have available today. Sometimes I wish I could turn the time back to the early 1980s, when I started my business career, to take with me the technical solutions of today. *What opportunities might have occurred to me with the help of social media?*

A book catches my attention: *The Surprising Purpose of Anger* by Marshall Rosenberg. I am immediately interested in the title because I am still struggling with mixed emotions, including anger, in my bid to make a satisfactory "as well as" decision. This book opens my eyes as it explains that my feelings are an important indicator of whether I am currently living in harmony with my needs. If I am, then I should feel good. If I am not, I could be sad, despondent, unconfident or angry. I have all these feelings at the same time. But what are my needs?

Through reading this book, I realise that it is important to get to know my needs, as often they can be subconscious. Only if I define my needs can I develop strategies to put them in context. This sounds like a treasure hunt.

My first task is to track my feelings. I understand mindfulness, so to track my feelings I need to avoid getting distracted by my thoughts. This is hard work, but all of a sudden I become aware of how much I am thinking and I realise that most of these thoughts are not constructive. They distract me and keep me from being present to recognise what I am feeling. I feel challenged by myself, but I accept this challenge because I am still in treasure-hunt mode.

In the beginning I find only small nuggets of wisdom, but they grow bigger day by day, although I cannot avoid the thoughts that still bombard my mind. At least I am getting better at realising that I am thinking, and identifying what I am thinking. This means I can say 'no' to my thoughts if they are not supportive, and instead focus on how I am feeling. I write my feelings down on sticky notes and put them on my wardrobe. I realise that my feelings are popping up in a constant pattern: disappointment, anger, frustration, excitement, curiosity. Now I need to start the second task: I need to find out why I am having certain feelings, by discovering what my needs are.

However, I am unable to unearth my needs. They are well hidden from me. I need help and remember the power of networking. A friend recommends a local "non-violent-communication" work group to me. They can be found in almost every city around the world. I join a group once a week and it helps enormously to practice with others and to share with them my feelings and possible needs.

When I am on my own, I consult a set of cards. The cards represent about 30 typical needs and by flipping through them I can quickly tell which of the needs resonate most with me. Looking at my situation at work, the needs that I identify are recognition, fairness, development, safety, belonging and freedom. These are a lot of needs, but they help me to develop a plan over the next couple of weeks. Finally, I know what my "as well as" solution will look like in alignment with my needs. I will reduce my working hours to three days a week, allowing myself freedom, safety and a sense of belonging. I will use the other two days to become a business coach and change expert, satisfying my need for development. This is something I have always wanted to do but never had the time for. It also fulfills my desire to foster recognition and fairness. I am convinced I will not have a lack of customers because I am not the only one out there working for the right company but for the wrong boss.

Today: 2021 Looking back, I am grateful for the fact that I have been able to live a life that has been so varied and surprising. Not everything has been perfect, but everything has been enriching. My "as well as" plan has worked out nicely and I have had the chance to help many people deal with change in their lives. I have encouraged them to drop the victim role and find their own solutions for a satisfying life. For myself, I identified a need to use my time wisely and this has very much been a determining factor in my behaviour.

I thank my parents for having been brave enough to make that big change in the summer of 1969 with two small children, not knowing what to expect, far away from their family and friends. All that, at a time when travelling and even long-distance phone calls were incredibly expensive. They gave me freedom and the psychological safety to grow and develop. Without that move I might have not learned so many of the interesting lessons that made me the person I am today: from the ability to reframe situations to being able to trust in life.

I also thank all the people in my network who have shared and created many milestones in my life. I thank them for their trust in me, their support, and for helping me to grow and shine. Believe it or not, I count that difficult boss among my milestone people. He also helped me to grow and shine, albeit in a painful way. But sometimes pain can be a catalyst that makes us take bold steps in a new direction.

Death... and Life

By Susan Devine

Death... and Life

*"Within a few years I would lose both Mom and Dad,
observe several supernatural occurrences,
and receive my own cancer diagnosis."*

My life has been unusual. My parents were born and raised in small towns in the United States, but my father's career led him abroad. As a result, my brothers and I lived in nine countries before coming back to the US for college at the age of 18. I got used to change, and loved experiencing the distinct cultures, peoples and ways of life, as I was discovering my own. I pursued a career in hospitality and continued to travel the globe. More importantly, I married my soul mate, who has become my partner in life, and together we have raised two wonderful boys.

What I'd like to share here is my experience with death. I did not think much about death until I was 40, when Mom was diagnosed with terminal breast cancer. Within a few years I would lose Mom and Dad, observe several supernatural occurrences, and receive my own cancer diagnosis. It was during this time that I began to develop my spiritual beliefs and adjust my life priorities. I now believe there is life after death, which is very reassuring. Death also teaches us how to live, and my search for understanding has led me to realize that our lives are most fulfilled when we love, forgive and actively practice compassion.

Living without fear

Mom was only 72 when she called with the terrible news that she had stage-four breast cancer. We all assumed she would live to 100. Her mother died just three months shy of the century mark and there was no family history of cancer. At the time of her diagnosis we were living in Mexico City. My boys were six and eight, and we visited my parents in Palm Harbor, Florida about twice a year, but decided to move to Miami to be closer to her. I started reading books to prepare for the inevitable: Deepak Chopra's *Life after Death*, Elizabeth Kubler Ross's *All About Dying* and *The Possibility of Reincarnation* by Brian Weiss helped me begin to form my own spiritual beliefs about death, and life after death.

Mom lived for almost ten years after receiving a terminal diagnosis. She spent her final three years in home hospice and we visited her often. It was difficult to watch her decline, but she handled it in a matter-of-fact way. I would clean her in the shower, massage her swollen arm to reduce the lymphedema, and bandage the grotesque skin wounds on her bare chest. Initially, it was difficult to see and do, but with repetition I learned to accept her deteriorating body and come to terms with the inevitable end result. Sometimes the slow dying process is a blessing in disguise.

It surprised me that Mom had no fear of dying even though she didn't believe in an afterlife. Her desire to continue to live, even with an extraordinary amount of pain, was based on love. I realized how important our visits were, and that every moment of shared love is precious. Little did we know then that these shared moments would carry on after her passing.

Turning on to new possibilities

Before continuing, you should know about the microwave incident. I was 25 and living on my own in Caracas, Venezuela. Almost exactly 24 hours after a friend of mine died in a car accident, my microwave turned on, all by itself. I had no logical explanation for this, though I related it to my intense thoughts of my lost friend at that very moment. I was spooked for several days, but put it to the back of my mind. Several years later I recounted the incident to Mom and Frank, my boyfriend at the time and now my husband of 27 years.

Three weeks before Mom's departure, she was starting to see things, and the hospice staff told me this was a sign that she was beginning to transition from this life. I reminded her about the microwave incident and asked her to communicate with me once she had passed. She laughed at the idea, but did not discard the possibility.

Mom continued to enjoy our conversations, watch TV, talk on the phone, and eat double desserts for as long as she could. She still wanted to know everything that was going on in our lives. I remember wondering how she could possibly care about her children and grandchildren's daily activities when she had such little time left, but apparently just hearing how we were living our lives was all she needed. She continued to appreciate the "little" things in life. I was beginning to understand how every moment matters, and that life is a journey rather than a destination.

About ten days before Mom's passing we had an amazing conversation in the middle of the night. I was sleeping in the bed next to her, so it was easy to hear that she was talking in her sleep. I sat next to her and she immediately recognized I was there.

'Let's go, Susie,' she said, her hands and feet moving back and forth as if she were walking quickly.

'Okay,' I said, 'Where are we going?'

'Shopping,' she replied. Then after a brief pause, she asked 'Should we bring Dad?'

'If you want to,' I answered.

'What if he gets lost?'

'Don't worry, Mom, I'll take care of him to make sure he doesn't get lost.'

'Okay,' she said, 'but we need a meeting place.'

'Where should we meet, Mom?' I asked.

'In the middle aisle,' she said definitively.

'Okay, Mom, you go ahead and we'll meet in the middle aisle. What are you going to buy?'

She thought for a moment and then decided, 'Two of everything!'

Her hands and feet continued to move quickly back and forth and we were off shopping. We repeated this general scene a couple of times before moving on to a new theme. I was exhausted, but I felt this communication was possibly a part of her transition to the "next world," so I just went with the flow.

Mom had fallen back to sleep when suddenly she sat upright in her hospice bed with a quizzical look on her face. Her eyes were a clear blue, and she asked, 'Mischu?' – as if to say, 'is that you?' A moment later, she exclaimed more definitely, 'Mr. Mischu! Oh, wow!' Then her head dropped straight back with force; mouth open, eyes closed and all energy gone.

Right then, the TV turned on by itself, showing just static. She was motionless, and I thought she had died. I stayed frozen in my seat, waiting for something to happen. Then after a minute I saw that Mom was still breathing. I was relieved, but still afraid to move. I asked her if she was aware that the TV had gone on by itself, and she sleepily responded, 'uh huh'. I waited another moment then clicked off the TV. I lay awake thinking about what had just happened. I was no longer scared or spooked, but in awe, and I wanted to understand more.

The next morning Mom was in good spirits, but I assumed she would pass later that day. I encouraged family members to call, and she spoke coherently with family and friends. These were rewarding conversations, as we believed this would be the last opportunity to speak with her. I shared the story of our journey the night before with everyone in the family as well as several friends, and we were all amazed. My 16-year-old son, JJ, felt there were only three plausible explanations for "Mischu" and the TV turning on. According to him, it was either energy, a spiritual force, or I was lying! We laughed together as we discarded the third possibility, and agreed it was pretty darn awesome.

The hospice nurses didn't seem too surprised, as many of them had seen this type of activity before. Apparently, it is common for doorbells to ring, electric appliances to go on, pictures to fall, etc. when someone is on their deathbed or has recently passed. Why don't more people know this? The nurses told me it is not very common for a family member to witness these events, but they assumed it was because I was open to the possibility of spirit connection and would therefore be accepting of what I might see. When the microwave had turned on 30 years previously, I became aware, but was not ready to accept. After this experience with Mom, I was excited and ready to learn more.

Mom made a conscious decision not to eat or drink and she was now prepared to die. She went for nine days without food or water and it was painful to see my mother slowly withdraw from this life. It was hard to know what to talk about, but I knew my presence was important and somehow the time passed very quickly. Mom had recently written a story of her life and she appreciated hearing me read it, adding my personal comments along the way. I also read her a story that my son, Cooper, had recently written in school. It was about his trip to outer space. He was scared to go but had no choice, and in the story, he mentions missing his Dad's pancakes. At that point, Mom laughed. She was hearing every word and enjoying the story, just three days before her passing and six days since having any food or water.

I cried myself to sleep most nights and was busy taking care of Dad, providing daily family updates, along with handling essential work emails and phone calls. But when I was with Mom, I knew that was where I needed to be and was fully present. Mom had always told me 'patience is a virtue'. I was finally catching on through her example. Who says parenthood ends once our children become adults?

Mom passed away at 3:07 EST on February 13, 2012. This was 12:07 PST in Silverton, Oregon, where Mom grew up, and on that day at that exact time her hometown girlfriends were gathering for their annual reunion. It seems implausible to me that this timing is coincidence. I believe Mom was able to choose her day and time of death.

It would take me too long to recount the numerous "coincidences" that followed Mom's passing. On at least ten meaningful occasions her favorite song, *It's a Wonderful World* by Louis Armstrong, suddenly played unexpectedly, and I firmly believe it was Mom's way of sending a message for me to hear and know. I smile, cry, reflect and give thanks every time I hear that song. Yes, even in the midst of chaos, uncertainty, sadness and despair, I believe it is a wonderful world.

I hugged my boys and we cried together. There was nothing left unsaid, and through Mom's passing, I learned about the real possibilities of life after death.

In the years that followed, I went back to a very busy lifestyle. Then, on December 21, 2016, I was hit with my own breast cancer diagnosis. I had accepted Mom's death and understood that there was an afterlife of some shape or form, but I was certainly not prepared to venture into my own. I was only 54 and had so much more life to live. More importantly, my husband and boys still needed me. It was at this point that I questioned my busy life, and suggested to myself that it was time to let go of my success-driven focus and redefine my priorities.

The hardest part of my diagnosis was the uncertainty. Was the cancer already in the lymph nodes? How aggressive would it be? How would my body respond? What was within my control? Mom had always told me that if faced with breast cancer at a young age, I should get a double mastectomy to reduce as much as possible the risk of it spreading. This also allows for full reconstructive surgery. Having lived through Mom's experience, it was easy for me to know what to do to when faced with my own diagnosis and over the years I have given the same advice to multiple friends who have faced similar circumstances. I keep my fingers crossed that my cancer doesn't come back, and feel blessed to have learned what we often hear but rarely understand – life is fragile and should not be taken for granted.

Dealing with Dad

Frank and I decided to design and build a home in the mountains of Asheville, North Carolina. Although neither of us was retired, we could work remotely and this was where we decided we wanted to live, possibly for the rest of our lives. It was a good choice, though for the next year we continued our hectic lifestyles with significant work responsibilities, constant travel and activity. It was the experience of Dad's passing that finally taught me how to slow down.

Living at home in Florida without Mom had been difficult for Dad and there had been several occasions in which we feared we were going to lose him. I was able to drive or fly in to help regularly, but it was a roller coaster. We decided to move Dad up to an assisted living facility in Asheville that was within a few minutes' drive of our home. I could visit him every couple of days but it still wasn't easy. When I was traveling, Frank would not go to Mexico City for his business in order to assume the family caretaker role. Despite these challenges, it was a blessing to be with Dad throughout the last year of his life.

Of course, it didn't always feel like a blessing. Dad was in and out of the hospital at least seven times in his last six months. He refused to accept the fact that he needed help to go to the bathroom or to do basic things he had always done on his own. His independence would be a detriment, and no matter how many times we asked him to ring the alarm around his neck, he wouldn't. He didn't seem too bothered that he would fall, unless he was forced to go to the hospital.

There were good days and bad days, and on the good days Dad would have everyone laughing. He was the only person in the senior living facility with an African Grey parrot and with his quick wit and charming personality, when he wanted to use it, Dad was well liked. He compared assisted living with college dorm living, though not quite as fun. He would often ask, 'Where's the party?'

Dad's dementia was sporadic, but his dependency was constant. During his last three months, it became harder for me to leave because I saw him going steadily downhill, and his concept of time faltered. There were occasions when I would call in from Cambodia, Mexico, Miami or elsewhere, and he couldn't understand why I wouldn't come over to see him. It was exhausting.

Dad was very good at hiding his dementia. He was exceptional at answering a question with a question to avoid having to give a real answer, and he knew everyone loved a joke. He used to tell me that people love to talk about themselves, so the best way to carry on a conversation is to ask questions, listen, and make them feel good about themselves. His advice was good.

Then, during one of his hospital visits, he became paranoid. He believed every staff member was out to get him and claimed he knew which nurses were bad by their mannerisms, tone of voice and facial expressions. We were not to trust anyone; he would spot all the hospital cameras and share what he thought was going on behind the scenes.

'Don't worry about the cameraman,' he said. 'Look for the person taking the photo of the cameraman. The guilty are usually not the obvious, and most are caught eventually because of their ego. Everyone wants their name in the paper and that is their downfall.'

I had not been told about Dad's intelligence training in the army, until I was 34. Mom and Dad had flown to Washington DC to take care of JJ while I was on a business trip, and it casually came up in conversation.

'We took JJ to the Pentagon, where your Dad used to work,' I remember Mom saying.

I was surprised to hear this, but I didn't ask many questions. After all, I thought, it had happened before I was born. While growing up, Dad worked for Goodyear Tires, and I was told this was the sole reason for all our travels. It was only after Mom's passing that I found Dad's handwritten autobiography in the desk, and realized how unique his life had been. It was a beautiful story of the first 30 years of his life, including growing up in the little town of Salem, New York, his college years, his intelligence training, and his time at the Pentagon. Unfortunately, his story was never completed.

I knew our time was limited and I wanted to know more about his life, and more specifically what he had done with his high-level intelligence training. Checking out of his last hospital visit, he told me he wanted this work mentioned in his obituary, and I realized that the advice he was giving me, as well as his paranoia, was related to his intelligence background. I asked him why he never told my brothers and me about it:

'For two reasons,' he replied. 'First, they teach you not to tell. Second, I am humble.'

Then, as typical with Dad, he diverted the question with a question. 'Susie, are you humble?'

I thought about this for a second and then told him I thought so, but probably not as much as I would like to think. He nodded knowingly in agreement.

Listening to the right messages
It was nice to be able to share our truths, and I once again felt our special bond that could never be broken. It also reinforced to me how important it is to have deep conversations with our loved ones before they die. These meaningful exchanges are critical for personal growth, closure, as well as the ability to move on.

Because Dad kept falling, we were told he would be better off in a nursing home where he could get increased care. After visiting various depressing facilities, I realized I did not want to move him. On the other hand, his assisted living facility told us he could not return unless we had 24/7 care for him. After close to an hour of back and forth conversation with Frank, measuring the pros and cons of each option, I said, 'Okay, it makes sense we move him to a nursing home."

At that exact moment, seven books fell from the built-in bookshelf in the den of our home office. I froze while Frank immediately went to pick up the books to replace them on the shelf.

'Do you think that is your Mom telling us something?' he asked.

'Yes, and her message is emphatically clear,' I replied.

The books fell from the shelf because I wasn't listening to the subtle messages telling me to keep him "home." We should all learn to listen to our intuition, even though it might be the more difficult route to take. Once we listened, another solution became obvious... hospice.

We sought out additional support from a local hospice dedicated to helping those who are dying. They provided Dad with a bed that could be lowered to the ground, so he wouldn't be able to get up in the middle of the night and risk falling. A nurse or aide visited him regularly to help manage his needs, and it no longer became necessary to take him to the hospital for every medical issue. Hospice care allowed him to stay in his senior living home and enjoy a high level of comfort.

Dad was not convinced of an afterlife and he was afraid to die. Unlike Mom, he didn't appreciate the "little things" in life, and would have preferred it all to end quickly. During the last months with him, I became aware of how unique we all are. I believe we get to know a person best when they are on their deathbed, or close to it, and we learn most about ourselves by taking the time to reflect upon these very special moments. I realized I had been very success-driven in my younger years because this was important to Dad and I wanted to meet his expectations. Now, it was clear to both of us that success was no longer a priority, or even important. In these last few months together, I learned to be present and patient, and I found the ordinary activities that we shared to be most extraordinary.

One of my most memorable conversations with Dad was about three weeks before his passing. It dawned on me that his fear of death, what I believed was holding him back from dying, was due to his need to be forgiven. I asked him if he needed to forgive or be forgiven, but he didn't know.

'Have you killed anyone?' I asked.

'No' he replied, 'but there were times when I was the second man in the boat, just behind the first who goes over.'

'Are you speaking metaphorically, or was this something that happened for real?' I wanted to know. We lived in Thailand during the Vietnam War when I was 6 and 7, so it was very plausible a scene like this could have occurred as part of an undercover mission.

He looked directly into my eyes and remained silent. He would not say more, and I was in a dilemma as to how to further help him. It then occurred to me that maybe I should forgive him, even though I didn't know what for.

I helped him to sit up and clearly stated, 'Dad, I don't know everything you have done, but I do know you have done many good things, including raising Mark, Murray and me, and I forgive you for absolutely everything that you need to be forgiven for.'

He looked at me incredulously and asked, 'Can you really do that?'

I responded confidently, 'Yes, and I have.'

He sighed in great relief. 'Thank you, thank you... you are blessed,' he said, lying back in the bed to rest peacefully.

In that moment, I witnessed the power of forgiveness and knew it would not be long before Dad was ready to move on. The next day I reminded him about the TV going on by itself during Mom's illness, and asked him to communicate with me after he died, if possible.

He smiled and said, 'Susie, I don't have that kind of power.'

Well, it turned out that he did! Just one month after Dad passed, while I was alone in the house and thinking about him before going to sleep, the living room TV suddenly switched itself on at high volume. Dad was a news-watcher, and here was the BBC celebrating the 50-year anniversary of Sesame Street, a show designed by parents to instill values in their children.

I knew this was Dad's way of telling me, 'I love you, and it's all good over here on the other side.' I smiled, and quietly thanked him for communicating with me. The past year had been a beautiful one of personal growth, and my wish for further validation of life after death had been granted.

The greatest lessons

About this time, I resigned from the hotel company where I worked, determined to focus my attention on meaningful activities. One of these has been volunteering for a hospice. I find that interacting with those close to death has allowed me to continue to grow. I share a few hours a week to help my hospice friends find comfort and joy, and come to terms with what it means to die. At the same time, I am building compassion and learning how to live. It is clear to me that material things are insignificant, while relationships are everything. Forgiveness is extremely important for the ability to pass on peacefully, and it is easy to love. Playing games is just as joyful at the age of 90 as it is at the age of 10, and lights will flicker while we talk about that "imaginary" animal or star.

The communication that I received from Mom and Dad in the midst of and following their deaths has given me confidence that there is an afterlife. I am not a religious person, so I had to see to believe. I was given the privilege of this experience through the bond of love and by being open to receiving. I realize there is a transition period before a person dies, and being present to "go with the flow" in conversation during this special time allows for the greatest learning. I am no longer afraid to die, and I am confident that my soul's journey will continue.

As I explore death, I continue to learn more about life. I believe that if we love, forgive, show gratitude, and practice compassion, we will live well... and die well.

Having witnessed the relevance and impact of my parents' stories, I have promised to write about my life before I get too old, and suggest everyone do the same. It is clear to me that we all have much wisdom to share. Life is precious, every moment matters, and love really is the foundation for life, in this body and beyond. Every shared experience can be rewarding, meaningful and inspiring. And yes, it *is* a wonderful world!

Healing the Female Ancestral Line

By Stella Photi

Healing the Female Ancestral Line

"The loss of children is a prevalent theme among the women in my family."

I was the first child to a young couple in London, first-generation immigrants from the small island of Cyprus, who had moved to the UK with their parents for a better life: to work hard, educate themselves and prosper, which was the way, and still is, for many immigrants. As the first grandchild I was adored by my grandparents and spoiled by my uncles and aunts. In my early years we all lived together in a big, three-storey Victorian house. I was enveloped with love by my parents and extended family.

My most special relationship was with my grandmother with whom I spent most of my time. I called her Mama-*yiayia* (*yiayia* meaning "grandmother" in Greek) as in my childhood innocence I felt she was my mother first and my grandmother second. She was a strong matriarch and kept the extended family together, doing her best for all of us. It wasn't until long after she died that I understood how challenging life had been for her.

Mama-*yiayia* moved with four children from her close-knit family in Cyprus, where they lived comfortably, to a strange and impersonal land, sacrificing her own comfort and way of life for a better future for them. My grandfather had a good heart, but she provided the ambition and drive for her children, making sure they had the best opportunities whenever she could.

My very early childhood memories feature my grandparents but not so much my parents. Not because they were absent, but perhaps as a result of spending most of each day with my grandparents as my primary caregivers. As I got older, my mother was less present and the bond with my grandmother grew even stronger. My parents were determined to have more children, so what followed were years of them both going through pain and suffering to make it happen. My mother's rare blood type brought on a condition in which her antibodies would attack the red blood cells of the baby when she was pregnant. This meant prolonged periods of time in hospital giving the babies blood transfusions. All of her subsequent three pregnancies ended with premature births and the deaths of her babies. All were given names as well as birth and death certificates.

My parents tried to shield me as much as they could from their heartache and what was going on, but I remember my father coming home from the hospital exhausted and sad. My grandmother kept a brave face on for me, but obviously felt the pain of her beloved daughter. I was an astute, intelligent child though, and by the age of eight could recite in detail my mother's condition using medical terms and explanations. However, somehow, when I look back I can't remember any of the emotions I had at the time. I have memories of my mother coming home from the hospital and lying in bed, broken and staring at the death certificate of my little brother, Andrew, born at six months. My uncle had bought me a puppy to distract me, but as I look back now, it seems obvious that all I really wanted to do was get closer to my mum and tell her that we would all be okay. But I didn't.

I heard many years later that my parents decided to stop trying for another child when I asked them if I wasn't good enough on my own for them. I cannot remember saying this or even thinking it, but we humans have a habit of suppressing painful emotions to protect ourselves. My body spoke, though. At the age of ten I developed alopecia, small bald patches appearing on my head. I think this is a clear indication that at some point the body eventually reacts to emotional pain, even in children.

Playing the game of life

The subsequent years were difficult. My mum was volatile, one moment showering me with affection and love, the next hurling verbal and sometimes physical abuse at me when I would trigger her by arguing or not following orders. Her temper was fierce and there was always some drama going on, either with her work or with one of her siblings. My father trod on eggshells around her, but I developed a strong will and would argue, disagree or ignore her wishes. This turned into resentment and the more she tried to dictate what I should do, the more I rebelled, often to my own detriment. From being top of my class and a grade-A student, I would skip homework and classes, hang out with friends she didn't like, and have boyfriends she did not approve of.

This, of course, is not unusual during adolescence, but the resentment simmered and extended to my father, who I felt never stood up for me or himself. I would hear him consoling her if I had been caught in a rebellious, adolescent act, and the anger and resentment would grow further. I knew she saw me as a disappointment, as I had been told many times, but I didn't care and I couldn't wait to leave the house and be able to do what I wanted, when I wanted. I felt suffocated and my will continued to grow, but I did play the game to some extent when I was at home, often lying about what I had done or where I had been in order to keep some semblance of peace and balance.

I left to go to university and a pattern began to emerge in my behaviour. I flitted from boyfriend to boyfriend, demanding complete adoration and losing interest as soon as I had it. At the time I told myself this was because I got bored easily and because each of my boyfriends didn't quite live up to all the qualities I was looking for. There was Roberto, who would pander to whatever I wanted but lacked ambition; Steve who had that ambition but was broody and troubled; Theo was handsome, polished and made me feel like a queen, but was too emotional; and Justin walked on the wild side and brought adventure into my life. I wanted the perfect bundle of all them, I would tell myself, surely there was someone out there like that?

Many years later I realised I had been looking for the gratification of being perfectly loved and adored so that I would feel good enough, not realising that I needed to build a love for myself first. Don't get me wrong, on the outside I was confident and self-assured, but in retrospect this was a cover for the subconscious emotions of a little girl who very definitely felt that she was not good enough.

I then met the man who later became my husband. I felt safe and secure around him and we had a lot in common, coming from similar backgrounds. It was a good fit as we both had similar aspirations and interests, and we developed a deep love for each other. He was different from my previous adoring suitors, as he found it difficult to show his emotions, so his love and attention was less demonstrable. The plan was to have three children. I wanted a larger family so my children would be part of a larger unit and have each other, as I had often felt lonely as a child. Not because I minded being on my own, but because nobody else could really relate to how it felt to be in my family.

My first pregnancy was difficult with a threatened miscarriage, but thankfully resulted in our healthy son being born. We had two blissful years with our baby boy, who was loved so much by all. This was followed by two miscarriages; the first of which I was told was very "normal", given the statistics of how common miscarriage is. 'Just try again,' I was told by my male GP, so my husband and I buried the deep sorrow of our loss and tried again.

The second miscarriage was more traumatic. It was unclear if the foetus was growing, so I was warned that I could miscarry at any time. I tried to go about my day-to-day business, holding down my job and looking after our toddler, but I was paralysed with fear. I held the foetus for four weeks, filled with dread and at the same time praying that I was carrying a healthy child. When it became apparent that the foetus had died weeks ago, I underwent a procedure to remove it.

'Try again,' I was told, but all I could do was think about the pain my mother went through, and how it affected me. I didn't want my son to go through the same thing. My mother told me not to compare our situations, that I wouldn't be the same as her, but I couldn't get beyond it. My husband wanted to try again and I felt like he didn't understand my pain. I felt unsupported and unloved. Again, the little girl inside wanted someone to put her first, and think about how she was feeling, though I didn't voice my needs. I shut myself down again, buried all the emotion, and distracted myself with my work.

Pushing the boundaries
My career took off and I was jetting around the world feeling very important and worthy. I was super-ambitious and worked for a company that rewarded my hard work with promotions and responsibilities. But old feelings re-emerged and I began to feel resentment towards my husband. Again, I thought he didn't appreciate me or love me enough, and he didn't feel my pain. I

asked him for a divorce, but his will was as strong as mine and he refused to move out or be separated from his son. I turned to my mother for support, but she told me I must sacrifice my happiness for the sake of my child. She said I needed help from a therapist and that I had been traumatised by my last miscarriage. With hindsight she was 100% correct, but at the time my resentment towards her just grew.

I had just started my business and wasn't in a financial position to leave the family home and pay for childcare, as my parents were helping me to look after our son. My mum stated that she would have no part in being used for something she didn't agree with. For several years my husband and I lived in the same house but did not have a healthy, loving marriage. We went through the motions for our son, and I dreamt about the day he would leave, so I could be free. I had the odd meltdown, but generally the atmosphere was polite, if cold. My relationship with my mother, however, deteriorated further. I felt continually judged by her, and I was angry that she wouldn't give me the unconditional love and support I so yearned for.

Everything changed the day my husband told me that he couldn't continue to live like this and he was moving out. I should have been elated, right? I had finally worn him down, won the battle, but I was filled with fear and emotion. I crumbled and started questioning if that was really what I wanted. The poor man was so confused and continued to prepare to move out until I eventually asked him not to. We talked and talked and shared our feelings. The situation changed from one of buried hurt and resentment to communication and understanding. We rekindled our love and this time we learned to speak to each other. I realised that he would not be able to understand my feelings and empathise if I didn't tell him how I was feeling. It was apparent that my usual line of 'he doesn't love me enough, otherwise he would just know' came from a place of naive immaturity and an insecurity in myself.

A new energy

Several years later, I was invited to visit a holistic retreat in Thailand as part of my work. I had a treatment called *Tsi Nei Tsang*, which is detoxifying for the organs but also good for emotional release. Something happened after that treatment and I had a complete physical and emotional breakdown. My lower back went into spasm and I released primal sounds of emotional pain. I cried continuously and was bed-bound for a few days. Luckily, I was in the right place for such an episode and the experts there supported me through my emotional and physical pain. I subsequently had a treatment with an energy healer during which I could feel the energies and spirits of my dead brothers and sisters, and my babies. Whether this was an actuality or not, it helped me reconnect to all that maternal trauma that both my mother and I had gone through, and to release some of it.

I called my husband from Thailand and told him I wanted another baby. This was met with silence. I could hear his mind working. 'All those years I wanted us to try again and you wait until I am almost 50 to tell me this?' But that wasn't what he said. By this time, we had both become much more aware of our communication style. Instead, he said he would think about it and we could discuss it on my return. We had the conversation when I got back, but by then I had had time to process the thought and realised that it was probably not the best move for us at that point, when our son was almost 15 and I was putting so much time and effort into my business. We bought a dog instead, whom we call our son, and we all love him as if he is.

Almost ten years later I am still processing those emotions that it took me so many years to recognise and release. Whenever

I see babies, whoever they belong to, I feel so much love. If I watch or read a story about a woman losing a baby or miscarrying, I can't stop the tears flowing. I feel it to my core, but at least I feel it rather than burying it. I am eternally grateful that we have our son, who is now 25 and whom we both love so much and are so proud of. I have also learned that when women bury deep emotional pain it is usually manifested physically in the female organs, such as the uterus, ovaries or breasts. I have seen this over and over again, whether it exhibits as cancer or other less serious issues, such as severe menstrual problems.

Running in the family

At this point I would like to mention my mother-in-law, who was a calm, humble and compassionate woman. I fell in love with her and she opened her heart to me, loving me as if I was her own daughter. Her life had not been an easy one, but by far the most agonising event of it had been losing one of her sons, at the age of ten, in a tragic accident. It was a senseless loss and I told her that I couldn't even imagine the pain she must have suffered. She told me that they'd had to get on with life and move on for the sake of her other son, my husband, who was a toddler at the time. Her husband told her she had to do it and she agreed, so they protected and cosseted their toddler, and didn't talk about their feelings or their deceased child any more. She buried her grief, stifled her tears and pain, and carried on.

My mother-in-law died of ovarian cancer in her mid-60s many years ago. I still miss her and she visits me in my dreams. I often ask myself how she could have released some of that pain and grief, and if she would still have been around if she had.

Which brings me to the story of my beloved cousin, Mary, who was like a sister to me when we were growing up. Mary was vibrant, strong and beautiful. She fell in love with, and married, a man who had MS. In her 30s she had miscarriages and a dangerous ectopic pregnancy, but she hid it all. Because her focus was to care for others, primarily her husband and members of his family, she put her pain and grief at the back of the queue. Everyone else came first. Mary died of breast cancer, aged 50, and all she ever wanted was to be a mother.

I believe that families carry ancestral trauma and mine is due to the loss of children, which has been a common occurrence among the women in my family, as has burying their emotional needs to keep their men happy and their children protected. I have become interested in shamanism and believe ancestral patterns and traumas can be healed, and I hope that some of the work and practices I am now doing will help heal my family.

My advice is to find ways to recognise pain, and then release it before it becomes something physical. With me it started when I lost my hair as a child, then in later years I suffered debilitating problems with my menstrual cycle. Luckily nothing life threatening, but nevertheless the pain impacted my life on many levels. I continue to try and heal my sacral chakra through practices such as yoga, affirmations and meditations. The sacral chakra is located just below the belly button and energetically relates to relationships with ourselves and others. I send love and healing to this energy centre, picturing white light permeating through that part of my body and leading upwards into my heart.

Although I was always regarded as outspoken, I had never spoken about my deep pain. Now I allow the white light to reach my throat, giving me permission to recognise and speak about the pain that sits deep within me. I have worked on my relationship with myself, knowing that I need to fully love and accept myself – and that I am enough. I was enough as that little child and I am enough now. I don't need constant adoration and attention from others to prove it. I can fully appreciate my husband's love on a deeper level without the constant demonstrations I searched for as a younger woman.

Recent circumstances, which I believe were orchestrated by the Divine, have brought me to live with my parents temporarily in my ancestral home of Cyprus. For the first time, I have shown an interest and curiosity in my mum's younger years, something I had previously only reserved for my dad, perhaps subconsciously shunning her. I have discovered more details about events in both my mother's and grandmother's lives, including the loss of unborn children by my grandmother that I was not aware of before, although somehow it did not surprise me.

I have learned about how personal sacrifice, unfulfilled personal dreams and a stoic family pride define my female ancestral DNA. I understand that it is my role to change this trajectory, to move forward with my mission in life, to live with joy and passion, and to understand that pride and sacrifice are not a validation of worthiness; that to love myself and know I am worthy is my right.

My last words are for my mother, to whom I dedicate this piece of writing in honour of our complex but deep relationship. After all these years I can recognise the loss and suffering she went through and I am full of compassion and love for her. I wish she could have worked through her own grief and not tried to protect me as much as she did, but I know she did her best. I also wish I could have been more aware of the pain she was carrying and caused her less stress, but I understand that we had to go through this for our own paths and learning in life.

As I sit here in my 50s and she is in her 70s, I want her to know that I am grateful for her strength and resilience, which I have been lucky enough to inherit. I want her to know that it is okay to recognise the pain and allow it to surface. I am full of compassion and love you, fully and completely mama.

COURAGE TO CREATE

HONORING INNER SELF

AUTHENTICITY

Education

COURAGE

REFLECTION

HOPE

spirituality

Wisdom

Evolving Beyond
Perceptions of Gender

By Uma Prajapati

Evolving Beyond
Perceptions of Gender

"I came across my own feminine wisdom, and it slowly unfolded as a sacred space for me."

Long hair, gold jewellery, tinkling anklets and bangles, silk saris, gentle laughter, a coy look toward the floor while talking to others – these were qualities I was brought up to cultivate as a well-behaved and admired woman in Indian society. I am standing today at the balcony of my house in Auroville, looking back at a life I left behind eons ago.

I joined Auroville at the age of 26 and it has become the grand love of my life. Auroville is an international spiritual township in South India dedicated to human unity. I came here in 1996 for a design project and fell in love with its vision. Back then there were 35 different nationalities living together as a community with no personal ownership. This fascinated me and I felt completely at home here. A dream called out to me and I could not go back to Delhi. My two weeks still have not ended.

I was the first-born girl in my family. Along with five sisters and a brother, I was born and raised in Gaya, a town in the state of Bihar in India. Gaya has been the seat of Buddhism since

Gautam Buddha found enlightenment there 2,500 years ago under a tree, and is now known as Bodhgaya. Though it has been central to Buddhists for millennia, today Bihar is not a very peaceful state. It has high violence and poverty rates and is known for being unsafe, especially for women. There are no longer any practicing Buddhists among the local population.

As a young girl, I always wondered how I would protect my father from the dowry system, which has a long history within Indian society and is followed rigidly in Bihar. A dowry is a lump sum given to a groom by the bride's parents upon marrying their daughter. It often creates a serious burden for the parents of the bride, putting them into lifelong debt. This pattern deteriorates the status of girls born into a family, as they are seen as a curse and a liability for fear of the effects of the dowry system. My father would have to work very hard to be able to marry his girls off. I had so many questions about the word "marriage".

I left for Delhi at the age of 21 to pursue design education at the prestigious National Institute of Fashion Technology. Upon graduating, I worked in Delhi as a fashion designer, becoming financially self-dependent at the age of 24. For me it was the privilege of a lifetime. I had waited for a long time to achieve this, but it did not last long. Soon after I started my first job, my thirst to find a deeper meaning in life began, my heart's yearning grew, and Auroville gently unfolded for me as a gift of grace.

The house of six sisters

I have been very sensitive to issues around women all my life. My parents' first child was a son and I was their second. As was common, they wanted a second son. Indian families are obsessed with having many sons. Parents see the son as security for their later years, as in Indian culture a son usually stays with the parents while girls marry and move to their husbands' homes with dowries. The son is also the absolute heir to the family business and name, and many Hindus consider a son to be an absolute must for furthering their lineage. This complicates the situation for both the girl child and her parents. While my parents were waiting for their second son, six daughters arrived. We became the famous "house of six sisters". I once asked my mother whether she had chosen to have each of us and she shut me up by saying, 'Never ever ask this question to any woman again.' Being a young child, I did not realise the enormity of that question then.

All the siblings in our family were creative, intelligent and hard working. Education was important to us all. In our household, though, there was a clear sense of increased attention toward my brother. He got a cup of rich cream while the daughters got a glass of simple milk. He received two eggs for breakfast while the girls made do with one. He received freedom and time to play, while we had to help our mother and spend time in the kitchen. Many things were mandatory for us, while he led a rather carefree life.

I left home at an early age to pursue my dreams and education, and did not really see my five younger sisters growing up. They did not know me much either, but knew of their *didi*, or elder sister, who lived in Delhi and sometimes came home on vacation. My family looked up to me as a path-breaker and an ideal in many ways. I was one of the lucky few at that time who had gone on to study at a prestigious school in the country, which was a dream for many in my hometown.

In my family, all six girls were exceptionally educated and our parents encouraged us to be strong and independent. My sisters all became respected and successful in their chosen fields. However, I did not see that my parents were particularly interested in their daughters' lives; rather it simply made my father proud. Things were always about him in one way or another.

Girls were to be the pride of their father, a bit like a royal commodity. We had to just survive being girls. We all became fighters and go-getters in some way. These life journeys and achievements had little meaning within the family unless they made our father proud. Home was all about him and the rest of us were just a meagre part of the interior.

A search for answers

I was in Delhi, living independently and making own my life decisions. My dream had come true. But when my first pay cheque arrived, I looked at that piece of paper and asked myself if I was truly happy. It only took a minute to answer: I was not. Next I began to seek answers to bigger questions. What is life? What is my highest purpose in life? Where do I wish to be? Happiness emerged as a very important feature in my life. I saw people running around me in search of it, but I was not sure they would find it in such a manner.

Then I came to Auroville in February of 1996 for that two-week design project. I landed in a forest without knowing anything about it, except that it is near Madras (now Chennai) and close to Pondicherry. Auroville is an international spiritual township that was founded in 1968 by Mirra Alfassa, also known as 'The Mother.' Auroville allows no ownership of any kind and the community lives and works together to realise the dream of human unity. After years of incredibly hard work, its once barren land now has several million trees and the community plants more every year. It is now a thick, lush, green forest with a conscious city blooming in its midst.

As soon as I arrived, I fell in love with this place. It was the perfect location to begin my quest for answers. I started to work in a unit called Auromode, a clothing company that is now called To Be Two. I felt that life was just perfect. I was given a place to sleep, a place to work and a place to eat. I had no other needs. The unit gave me a small remuneration to maintain myself, but I could not even spend that money.

Two years later, under a majestic tree, I founded a clothing company called Upasana with the dream of bringing India to Auroville through textiles. I had 2,000 rupees in my pocket – approximately 30 euros – and a dream. I became a humble caretaker of this unfolding. Very soon, Upasana was operational with textiles from 16 states within the country, and it was making a profit.

Following the tsunami in 2004, Upasana was active in supporting women in the fishing community. We worked with many different groups from farmers to silk weavers in Varanasi and an ecological campaign supporting women's empowerment. Upasana became a hub for social change and I became increasingly aware of how business could be an important tool for societal impact. I learnt design for social responsibility while working in the villages and my interaction with the humble cotton farmers changed my life and my perspective. The horrendously high level of cotton farmer suicides in India impacted me deeply, and my work as a designer shifted. My world was not to be the same and I ended up making big changes in my business and my life. In 2010, Upasana launched the Paruthi brand of organic cotton for the domestic market, and my journey toward "conscious fashion" began. We created an educational platform called The Conscious Fashion Hub, hosting and creating a conference each year.

The ownership of Upasana is collective. It does not belong to me alone. As an executive, I am one of the staff. Non-ownership was a new and awkward idea when we began and it continues to be novel to some. I have never lived in a scarcity mindset though. It is a gift from the divine and an aspiration from me to choose to be living and working in this space. Non-ownership gives me freedom and a vast range of expression, which is sacred to me.

Upasana is unusual and ahead of its time in many ways. When we began, nobody was thinking of organic clothing and people did not understand why it was even important. Upasana became a pioneer in many ways and our courage to act brought media attention from all over. So many projects grew out of our work, and between our community work and building a brand as a business, I was drowning in a sea of productive and creative leadership, but I did not know how to care for myself.

Accepting myself

During a leadership programme I attended in Auroville, I met Dr. Monica Sharma, who taught me about knowing and honouring myself in multi-fold ways. She has now been my teacher for more than seven years and, along with The Mother and Sri Aurobindo, she has guided me toward tools that have made my spiritual life more whole. These practices are efficient resources to help do the work one needs to do and enable us to shine towards our full potential.

Auroville truly changed my life and I am deeply grateful for the space I was given to work, eat and sleep in my early days there. I wanted to pay this gratitude forward in a tangible way by providing a place for others going through their own journey of self-discovery in Auroville. This thought gave birth to Rohini – a home for seekers. Rohini was built in 2013 as a space for volunteers. Many people come to Auroville and stay in guesthouses, unaware of how the community lives or interacts. My dream was to bridge this gap, which I experienced myself 25 years ago.

I happened to meet Claudia Roth in *Rohini* one day through a common friend. She has been instrumental in putting together this book and has become a catalyst to further growth for me. Rohini has been a home for many volunteers and also many

Aurovilians. Many people who live there during their volunteer days also end up becoming Aurovilians. Rohini helps newcomers to connect with Auroville and grow to understand its way of life. We have an open-house breakfast every Sunday morning and a weekly meditation gathering followed by dinner every week, open to all. I believe that we all have a need to connect with one another at a deeper level through a safe community space.

I have a deep trust in the Divine, a higher intelligence that is at work all the time. Auroville offers everyone time for contemplation and meditation and this has helped me realise that I have natural courage and wisdom. This was reinforced in the sessions I had with Monica, but I began to notice that my courage and wisdom was not easy for everyone to handle. A few years ago, I became aware that I often overwhelmed people. However, instead of fighting with myself and trying to "fix" this, I learnt to accept it and honour it as my own presence. This acceptance led to greater comfort and peace within my personal space.

I realised I needed a separate physical space while I worked on my inner space. I found that my bedroom was the place where I could be fiercely and unapologetically myself without threatening anyone. Even though I am in a relationship with my partner, Torkil, he understands this need and we maintain separate rooms. We have been together for ten years and share this graceful acceptance, which I consider a precious gift to myself.

Regular silence and contemplation has helped me to reflect on how my life can be relevant to myself and others. We very often live lives that are self-centred, as this is the most natural instinct to have as humans. Most often, after a point, this need for self broadens and a larger community or society becomes our family. Living in Auroville has widened my sense of family. Mine now contains more than 3,400 people of 55 different nationalities. This has quietly changed my way of thinking. It has become natural to me to think of how I can be of service to others and to the larger collective, while still honouring the feminine within me.

My own feminine wisdom has slowly unfolded as a sacred space for me. It was not about just being a feminist, but rather about holding the values of the Divine feminine. The whole universe is her family. Feminine leadership calls for a holistic approach towards all things, centering on a heart relationship, as the heart operates from a space of integrity and authenticity. I became more and more conscious of that space and began honouring the slowly unfurling wisdom of the sacred feminine within me as it began to shape my journey. I grew up conditioned by an Indian culture in which the feminine language was weak: passive and submissive. Luckily, I did not shy away from speaking my mind and did not fool myself by beating around the bush or playing diplomatic games.

Spending time in silence and regular meditation moved me toward increased clarity in both speech and thought, thereby better allowing me to shine my light. I have been running a few social projects and the Upasana clothing brand with a commitment to socially responsible business and real-life projects of empowerment. People often saw me as quiet and wise, but some were overwhelmed by my dynamic side. Yet all of these are facets of me. This complexity doesn't always make sense to people raised within a patriarchal background. We are yet to evolve into a society that thrives beyond simple perceptions of gender. Feminine energy has been subjugated in the east and commodified in the west, and in both directions it has been corralled into a non-empowered space. True honour and respect towards women need not be dependent on laws, upbringing or education. It can stem from possessing the humility to honour our own existence, honouring the Divine feminine from whose womb we are all born.

The Courage of Love, Faith and Hope

By Liliana Martins

The Courage of Love, Faith and Hope

"The trip to Africa was a return to the origins of my soul, the connection I spent my life yearning for."

Who am I today? What roles do I play and how many identities do I fit into this story called life?

Writing our own stories around big questions such as these can be a great way to heal, even though a lot of us do not take the time to do so, fearing it to be too self-centred. All I can say is that it worked for me, as I write to discover the person I am today: a product of my true essence as well as my family values, the culture I grew up in, the programming I received and the beliefs I have developed. I am a complex combination of experiences, places, languages, lifestyles and cultures.

I am Afro-Portuguese. My parents are from the Cape Verde islands and I was born in Portugal. I would have been a Maria if my mum had accepted my dad's suggestion. Thank God for her interference. I wonder how much my name has influenced my life?

I like to believe I was born to be different and that my purpose on Earth is to be remembered. Where I grew up, I was the only "Liliana," yet the rest of my name was my mum's full name. Sometimes I feel that along with her name, I carry with me her energy, her essence, her dreams and all that she wanted to be. My mum told everyone that I was just like her, but I did not like the way that made me feel. I wanted to be my own person. Parental bonds are some of the strongest we have and they are responsible for many of the life-changing decisions we make as we grow up. Our parents are probably the most important people in our lives as without them we would not even be here, on Earth, alive!

Times of tough love

My parents were very strict. I grew up in a tight family with six of us in the house. My dad's parents came from Africa – the Cape Verde islands – to live with us when I was four years old. They brought my eldest sister, Amelia, with them. We called her Yuka. Suddenly the household was busy and full of people. I remember the smell of *cuscus* and *cachupa*, two of the most traditional Cape Verdean dishes I can think of. I remember the singing, the dancing and the constant sound of African music. Often my grandad played guitar. We descend from a family of very famous Cape Verdean musicians.

Collectively much was happening as at that time Portugal was restructuring, moving from a dictatorship to a democracy. It was 1974 and I was too young to understand a lot, but I remember the soldiers marching on the streets with their guns up, with carnations inserted in the gun barrels as a sign of victory for the people.

In recent psychology sessions I travelled back to the age of four, to the deepest and the most important pain that I have stored in my body, mind and soul. I allowed myself, at the age of 50, to return to painful places and incidents that I had carried all my life, as if they were still happening. Such events as feeling like a victim of circumstances when I was physically smacked as a child; the disempowered decisions I made throughout my adult life in relationships, because any expression of authority would take me to a place of fear and submission, harking back to the restrictions placed on me by my parents and grandparents. Despite living in a loving family, punishment and smackings came with the culture of raising children.

As a child, when we received visitors in the house, we were not to be seen. I used to love it, as this was our opportunity to disappear without my mum knowing where we were. We had an hour or two of freedom. I loved going to my friend's house to play, being outside and seeing people, connecting.

As I grew up to be a young woman, I realised that to my parents, my sister and I were "untouchables." No boy was allowed to even touch our arm. I was scolded and punished for allowing my fellow football colleague to just hold my arm. We were brought up to be almost immaculate, or that was my perception.

Maybe it was circumstance. I grew up in a blended family of six. My mother's last child was stillborn, and sometimes I felt that the pain of losing her latest child forced my mum's focus onto me. For most of my life her excessive love and attention suffocated me. But I understand her now. I have forgiven all the pain, and the love we have for each other allows us to have a wonderful relationship. It took me a long journey of therapies, soul-searching tears, arguments and rebellion, but it was all worth it.

From my mother I received my spiritual background as a child, the teachings and the practices she shared. From her career as a nurse she taught us to look after ourselves through the conventions of the western medical world. She also taught us her African background of healing medicines, teas and compresses, oils and herbs. She taught us to stick together as siblings. She smacked my brother and me, yet she would not allow my dad to touch us, defending us fiercely.

Supportive siblings

In 1982, when I was 12, my family moved away from our home. I was excited, but at the same time I missed my old friends, old home and old habits. My emotional body was in conflict but the physical and mental parts of my body were in total harmony.

I had trained as a figure skater from the age of five until that point, but when we moved I stopped, as our new home was far from the training facilities. I missed skating so much. Training made me feel good and gave me purpose. Competitions and skating events were part of my upbringing and suddenly they were gone. I felt a void. Although I had competed from an early age, I never believed in myself enough to be a champion. Maybe I was too afraid to excel, to shine my light, because the fear of not being accepted or liked was greater than my ambition I had to better myself. Nevertheless, any dreams of skating were now gone.

By this time, my sister and I had grown to be very close. We supported each other in everything and grew even closer emotionally through the changes. One way to cope with everything that was happening around us was to play football and we joined the local team. Everywhere we went, we dragged our brother along. My brother was quieter and never seemed to complain about much. My mum wanted us to stick together through thick and thin, and we did. Family unity was important to my parents, and we held tight to it.

By the end of 1988, my sister, whom I loved dearly, left to go to England and live with her aunt, leaving another void in my heart. However, I was actually accustomed to this feeling as my dad left us to go to work all the time. During our childhood,

Dad was not present for long periods of time. He worked for German ship companies and went away often, spending only about two to three months a year at home. I grew accustomed to his absence. Only as an adult did I come to realise the impact that this had on my relationships with men.

Growing up, I believed my mum's stories about my dad and about men in general, as he was not around enough to get to know him and ask him my own questions. I grew up to be independent, to not rely on men but stand on my own and to not allow them to rule my life. I thank God again, this time for my rebellious personality. Although my mum's programming was well implemented in the computer of my brain, and the repetitive behaviour I witnessed suggested default reactions, my spirit rebelled. Many of the things I was told did not resonate in my heart. My soul's essence screamed to be freed from all those rules, beliefs and ideas that did not serve me. I left the nest when I was 18 in search for the real me.

Freedom and dance
I followed my sister, Yuka, to England, where I met a Brazilian guy with whom I had a relationship for three years. His sister taught me how to dance and we used to go out and dance the night away. The sounds of salsa, samba and all the Latin vibes filled my soul with happiness. I joined a Brazilian dance group in London. I loved being part of this colourful, exuberant group, and this was around the time when Ricky Martin had really put Latin dance on the map.

One of our group's most memorable performances was for the first wedding anniversary of Princess Caroline and Prince Ernst of Hanover, in the year 2000. When we had finished our performance, we were invited to join the party. There was a band playing salsa music and to my surprise, I was invited to dance by a man who I realised was Prince Albert of Monaco. Prince Albert of Monaco! We danced and when the song finished, he asked me what I wanted to drink before leaving to fetch me a rum and Coke. I suddenly felt very nervous. I felt so awkward, so out of place, so out of my element, that I let myself be pulled back onto the dance floor by someone from our group. When Prince Albert came back, I was dancing with my friend and the Prince was left standing on the periphery.

I understand now that my emotional body was very young, and my insecurities sabotaged the moment for me. My psyche simply could not believe that a Prince had asked me to dance. Deep inside I felt a lack of self-worth regardless of the fact that the universe was manifesting and gifting me such wonderful experiences. I will always wonder to myself 'what would have happened if I had stayed put?'

I discovered so much freedom in England. I got a job as a nanny and I studied English in the evenings. Mastering languages came easily to me as I had grown up speaking two of them; my parent's native language from the Cape Verde islands, which was a Portuguese creole, and Portuguese itself. It was so easy to become a Londoner; I fell in love with London!

While I was living there, I began to travel to other places, first as part of my job and then for leisure. My first trip out of England was to Greece, which was another dream come true as I had long wanted to visit this land thanks to my interest in studying ancient civilisations. For the next few years I continued exploring Europe, visiting friends and family.

A journey for the soul
Travelling with the Brazilian dance group, one of my first performances was in Tanzania on my first visit to Africa. What a powerful experience that was for my soul. I felt the pull of the

land – the Africa of my ancestors. I met people from the Masai tribe on the streets and felt the power of their way; how they walked, how they looked, the way they dressed. They are warriors and they exude respect, power and beauty. I felt so attracted to them as a people. It was almost as if I belonged there with them. I wish I'd had the courage to explore more, but I felt intimidated by the powerful respect I had for them.

Africa was like that. It was a powerful continent to visit. In 2,000, I went back there with my family. We decided to travel to the Cape Verde islands, where my parents had come from. They had not visited the islands for 40 years, and I was there for the first time. My brother decided not to come with us, choosing instead to follow his girlfriend on a trip to Brazil. I think we all felt somewhat hurt by this, having been brought up in such a spirit of strong family unity, but nobody questioned it. I realise now that as a unified family we are also very accepting and forgiving. Or perhaps we just suffered in silence. I will never know. How do love and hurt intersect?

This trip to Africa was a return to my roots; to the origins of my soul and the connection I had spent my life yearning for. In Africa, I faced the questions of "who am I?" and "who am I becoming?" This land was the vital component that helped me understand the nature of my relationships with others. Ultimately, it taught me the meaning of life.

Days of my lives
The same year of our Cape Verde trip, I opened up to a completely different way of loving and seeing love. I suddenly had new feelings and deep connections that I had not experienced before, and could not understand. As a result, I searched for meanings to new questions and decided to look for answers down the path of past-life regression therapy.

During my second session of past-life regression therapy, I was taken to a place that felt so real, and yet so much like a dream that it is hard to believe I was in a conscious state. It was a cinematic experience. In my mind's eye the world was split into two screens and they played a film that had a script that made sense to my heart even though my mind had to work to comprehend and accept it.

The lesson I was being taught was that not everything in my life could be seen as black and white. I came to learn that I am part of a family, a country and particular time for a reason. I had to accept that people show up in my life with purposes that do not necessarily make sense in the present. I realised that the soul is searching for meaning in this lifetime, but that meaning might require many threads from other lifetimes to come together before it makes sense.

Within this search I discovered the concept of soul mates and the connections between twin souls. This opened up a new world of possibilities; an understanding of purpose, and meaning with regard what we are doing on Earth. If my family and friends thought I was deep before, now they thought I was crazy.

I entered a new world of energy, higher connections and perceptions; a world of emotions, power, sensitivity, karma, contracts, agreements, forgiveness, compassion, patience, knowledge, ancient wisdom, amazing encounters, self-discovery, self-love, self-acceptance, release, joy, happiness, courage, strength, discomfort and growing emotional and spiritual pains.

I enthusiastically searched for mentors who could discuss with me the meaning of life. I went on workshops for healing the heart, the body and the soul, and alongside all my searching, I kept travelling the world and I kept on dancing, even teaching dance fitness classes.

Love, faith and hope

In the midst of this time of questioning and discovery, in 2017 the Grenfell fire happened in London. I lived across from this 24-storey building and on a summer night in June, I spent eight hours watching from the beginning to the end as a solid concrete building I had been familiar with for 22 years burnt to ashes, taking with it the lives of 72 residents. I saw people dying. I saw people trapped between fire and a high-rise window. I will never forget the orange backdrop, the shadows, the shape of a body moving back and forth, and the window, too high to offer any solution other than death.

The experience of that night sent my vision of life – my spiritual, emotional, physical and mental perception of my existence – to a totally different level. I tried to express what it had made me feel in a song I co-wrote with a friend, called *Grenfell, We Won't Fall*.

More than ever before, I now knew that life was to be lived on a daily basis, every moment of every day was to be cherished and people in one's life should be valued and loved all of the time.

It is so easy to go to bed thinking that you are going to wake up the next day – we don't even realise we are taking it for granted – but there are no guarantees of tomorrow.

What I have found in this journey called "life" is that in love there is great pain sometimes, yet there can also be faith and hope. As long as we are united, we are well.

We need love because without finding love in everyone and everything there is no purpose in the journey. It is necessary to love ourselves first, so we can then love one another.

We need to learn to have faith so we can put our trust in God or the inner wisdom that resides with us. In doing this, we can discover that the Universe will always provide the answers to every circumstance and challenge.

Hope encourages us to overcome obstacles and enables us to accept pain as part of experience, growth, and the expansion of our being. Happiness and joy should always be our main goal.

I had a mentor who used to say, 'When you are going through hell, don't stop to watch what is going on around you. Keep going!' As long as you can focus on the exit, you can find love, faith, hope... and a light at the end of the tunnel.

Being Alive

By Elodie Baran

Being Alive

*"I successfully freed myself from the real brace
and also from the brace I had created in my mind."*

My story started when I decided that it was time for me to be born. After four years of marriage, the parents I chose had accepted the fact that they wouldn't have children. Then my mother started to feel sick and had stomach pains. The doctors had all told her that she could not be pregnant and she was far along when it became undeniable. She was afraid; she had been taking pills that were not recommended during pregnancy and it was too late to get an abortion. There was a life force in me that told me to hold on. I did just that, and this attitude of "holding on" has helped me to bounce back from difficulties I have faced in my life.

So, here I am, 50 years later, ready to give birth to these pages and share with you the story of a girl, raised by loving parents in a bourgeois environment, looking for herself. I hope it can inspire you in finding your own tools to enjoy the life you desire.

Object versus subject
I have very few strong memories of my childhood. I was the oldest of my siblings, including my cousins. It seems in my early

childhood I was the leader of our group. I had a tendency to walk on the edge and climb on roofs, which resulted in bedtime stories that related how badly we had behaved and how we would be punished. At the same time, I was very shy and scared to speak to anyone, or even pick up the phone when it rang.

The wishes of my father always came first and we had to obey. My father had raised his brother, who was 12 years his junior. Four decades later he applied the same methods he had used on my uncle with my brother and me. We had to be the best and we had to be obedient. My father had a temper and could not accept that I could have thoughts and desires for myself that were different from his. I was never appreciated or good enough. For many years, I shut down my intuitions and my real aspirations, and just obeyed.

I was born with a double scoliosis that was detected when I was two or three years old. I remember going for check-ups at the hospital each year until the beginning of puberty. At the last visit, the doctors suggested that I undergo an operation to attempt to control the twists and curves of my spine. My parents were devastated and looked for any other solutions that could prevent this surgery, in which the spine is straightened using rods attached with screws, hooks and wires. This was something I had nightmares about. The alternative was to visit a hospital near the sea where I would be attached to a bed or wear a Milwaukee brace. My parents chose the latter. I wasn't asked. I had no say in the decision.

This felt like imprisonment. I was a young girl and my parents were in full control. After four hours of consultation at the Saint Vincent Hospital, I left with my first Milwaukee brace. This is among the most restrictive of back braces. It runs from the pelvis all the way to the neck and includes a pelvic corset, a thoracic pad, a neck ring and a rib pressure pad. I was ten years old, shy and totally unprepared and unsupported for this experience that lasted eight years. Neither the doctor at the hospital nor my parents ever thought of how this brace could affect my self-esteem, my body image and my overall quality of life. I felt treated as an object. Once when I went to the hospital for a check-up, I entered an examination room full of doctors discussing my spine. I felt detached from my body. "Elodie" did not exist anymore; I was reduced to a body with a curved spine that was being treated with a Milwaukee brace. I was an object to fix.

To be effective, I had to be in my Milwaukee brace for 23 hours each day. I had only one hour of freedom to wash myself. I could not tie my shoelaces anymore and used to break my little toe quite often, as I could not see my feet. I had to learn how to sit again and get up from the bed. I swapped my clothes for loose ones – clothes to hide the brace. I put on a brave face and I even joked about it and made my schoolmates laugh, but inside I was lonely. I felt like a circus monster, either pitied or treated as a freak. As I was well trained, I never complained or rebelled even when spending the summer at the beach.

Stages of freedom

When I turned 18 years old, all restrictions were lifted. I could do anything in line with my parents' expectations. That year I got rid of the brace and got the keys to a studio flat 15 minutes' walk from my parents' home. Suddenly, I had my freedom. It was oddly disturbing for me: where were my boundaries? Though it was exciting living by myself, I also felt abandoned.

The flat was in a little mews with about eight other apartments. I had a small garden and would babysit for my neighbours. The freedom scared me more than anything. I was still the shy little girl, studying as best I could and having dinner with my parents every night. I went to some events and organised parties, though

I did not drink nor smoke. I created a brace in my mind and I would not let it go; a shield that made it more difficult to truly connect with people and myself.

At the same time, my parents stayed too connected to me. My house became an extension of theirs. They had the keys and didn't recognise boundaries. One day when I was away, my mother took some friends to visit my place without my knowledge. I was shocked. I felt my privacy had been violated. It was time to make a break.

When I finished my degree in Paris, I had the opportunity to get another qualification in public relations in London. I jumped at the opportunity, left my flat and embarked on a one-and-a-half-year stay in the UK. Suddenly I was a stranger in a new country with a blank page to write. It was true freedom for me. I could be myself, choose my path.

I really enjoyed life as a student in London. I shared flats, got a part-time job and even had a relationship. I had an active social life and met people from all over the world. It seemed for me that suddenly the world was calling me. I could be whatever I wanted. After graduation, I looked for a job, though I wasn't sure what I wanted to do. At this cue, my father called me back to work with him. I felt obliged to obey and returned to France.

Suddenly, I was back in my unconscious brace. I did not belong. I was back in a box with codes that I hated – a dress code, a speaking code, a thinking code. I was totally off kilter and I sometimes wondered when driving, what would happen if I hit a wall. Unprepared for this change in me, concerned and not knowing what to do, my parents sent me to a psychiatrist. There I came to understand the influence of the brace and the effect it had on the development of my personality. I was disconnected from my emotions and my intuitions. I was blind.

At 25 years old, having not really lived during my teenage years,

I was just entering my first "adolescent crisis". My education of obedience still kept me on the right side, but with a little craziness. In a rebellion against my father's racism and to feel part of a group, I became friendly with an employee in my father's company who was from a French Caribbean island. In London, I had a Jamaican boyfriend and I felt related to the community. I also felt most free when dancing to Latin Caribbean music. My parents frowned on this association. One day, my father told me that he had seen me in the supermarket with my boyfriend and decided to ignore us. I felt shame and rejection.

Despite the pain of this realisation, I was desperate to conform to what my parents and society wanted. I realise now that I did not have a choice whether to be conformist or not. I believed it to be an obligation. I had to get married to the right person and have children and a high-income job with responsibilities. I was struggling to find "Elodie". I had lost her along the way.

One day, a violent sexual encounter sent me over the edge. The situation was so shameful that I felt I had left my body and was looking at myself from above. It was one of the strangest and scariest experiences of my life. I needed help. I had terminated the previous psychiatry sessions, as I thought I understood myself, but I was far from having the tools to be in the driver's seat. Several months before, a friend had recommended a therapist who used group therapy to help patients reconnect with their emotions. I went without knowing what to expect and the intensity of the session triggered all my defences. I suddenly realised how much I kept inside. Listening to the group express their emotions was a shock to my system.

At one session, I shared how during my 17th year I had cried almost every day for no apparent reason. I had not understood what was happening to me. I had been alone with no one to guide me through this intense feeling of pain and sadness.

The therapist explained to me that crying was a sign of good health and a path toward healing. I felt relieved to know that it was normal to express emotions. It took all those years of ups and downs to understand my emotional roller coaster.

Becoming *l'étranger*

For the first time, I disobeyed and left my father's company to look for a job in events. I used all my creativity and managed to get work in a travel company thanks to my knowledge of databases. Working in travel made sense. My parents and I had often taken unusual trips, like a cruise in the Mediterranean, or to Odessa during the Gorbachev years. Each summer, we would travel around the world for three to four weeks, and by the age of ten I had already visited the west coast of the USA and Peru. These big adventures impressed me so much that when I decided to find a new job, I looked abroad.

Though happy living in Paris, my travel job became dull. I was creating amazing programmes for clients that I never had the chance to experience myself. I was looking at beautiful destinations and activities in a dark corner of an office. My typical day was: up at 7am, take the tube, go to work, finish by 7pm, come back home, have dinner, watch a film, go to bed. "*Metro, boulot, dodo,*" as we say in French. Winter was the worst. I suffered during cold weather and short daylight hours, and was desperate for a change. I dreamed of sun on my skin, luxurious vegetation and a slower pace of life with an exotic boyfriend, as my relationships in Paris were going nowhere.

One day I said 'enough' and looked for opportunities to fulfil my dream. And there was Costa Rica. It was one the quickest decisions I have ever made in my life and it was completely for myself, even if it did take me completely out of my comfort zone. I had no clue where Costa Rica was. Spanish was a foreign language to me that I had only related to through salsa dancing. I was leaving for the unknown. For once, I trusted life and the life force I knew I had in me.

My journey to Costa Rica was hectic and emotional. I sold up, packed and moved out in only three weeks. On the last day in my flat with no furniture, no clothes, I was momentarily traumatised. How could I have taken such a radical decision? I arrived at the airport with my suitcase, a trunk and my cat. My legs were shaking, my heart was breaking and the cat was meowing. It was a painful picture. Not at all the one I had expected. To add to the challenging journey, I was travelling ten days after the 9/11 attacks on the Twin Towers in New York. Security was very high and I had to go through a detector carrying a crying cat in my arms.

Finally, I arrived in San José. The heat and the light hit me when exiting the airport. I was awash in colour and vibrancy. I woke up every day with the sun and to the sound of the river in my backyard where a little squirrel visited. I had breakfast in my luxurious, miniature garden with flowers and plants of all colours. Each day I ate a different fruit that was so fresh it melted in my mouth. I worked in a travel agency that was located on the corner of the road in an old house overlooking majestic trees. I was able to experience all the activities that I was offering to clients: walking in a coffee plantation, smelling the roasted coffee; zip lining in the trees like Tarzan; enjoying the hot bath at the foot of the Arenal Volcano; lying on one of the several beaches on the Pacific and Atlantic coasts. After work, I went to Latin dance classes and met new friends. I returned to a more mindful and less stressed life. Each day was a new beginning and new discovery. As they say in Costa Rica, everything was *pura vida*.

It took me four months to speak Spanish and eight months to

be fluent. It was frustrating not to be able to communicate properly. I had little contact with my parents and friends, as the internet was still a recent invention. I had to create a new home with new friends and a new way of life. The experience was worth the fear and doubts I encountered, as it created who I am now and demonstrated my abilities.

Back to reality

My Costa Rica adventure lasted for 11 years. Eventually I became bored in my job and was still looking for my Prince Charming. Was my desire real or was I still bowing to the weight of society's expectations? A poisoning dissatisfaction still ran in my veins. How could I be dissatisfied living in paradise? It seemed I still believed that a man and a family were to be my purpose in life. These imprisoning beliefs were still in my head. I needed to go deeper to find "Elodie".

I realised that I missed the European culture, so when I got the offer of a job in London that allowed me to reconnect with my first "self," I took it. London was my home. London had been my first experience of freedom – it was the city of all possibilities and I had great hope of finding love.

I arrived there with great expectations, though nothing went as planned. It was difficult to find a flat near my work and where I could live with my cat. Then I suddenly became the "mother" of a teenager when my goddaughter decided to finish her studies in UK and I became her guardian. For five years things marched along well, then everything went downhill. My cat died after 18 years with me, I felt harassed in my job and no longer found any meaning in what I was doing. I was also still very much single.

I left my job without any backup. I simply could not work anymore. I was physically and morally exhausted. I lost confidence in myself and lost the last anchor I had. Each time I had changed a job in the past an opportunity would open up, but this time I was facing my oldest and darkest fears. I felt I had nothing: no job, no relationship, no project. I decided that I had to reformulate my desires, my dreams, my sense of purpose and, lacking answers, I fell into a nearly unbearable depression. The only thing that felt real to me was the life force that brought me into this world.

I searched for help, connecting with people who had similar experiences or were thinking in a similar way. I looked into activities that I had never allowed myself to do before. I nourished myself with travel, dance, food and my support network. I decided to date. I was not a fan of dating apps, but as I could not meet people organically, I found the courage to make that jump. I was alive, I was moving, I was sociable and I discovered a great community of conscious people who accepted me with open arms. With practice, I again learnt to connect with my intuition and my own desires. I learnt to let go and trust what life will bring to me when I am open to receive. I challenged my beliefs and I protected my bubble. I released my anger and I decided to be responsible for my own satisfaction or dissatisfaction. I decided to give to nobody the power to make me feel bad or good about myself.

Where am I now? I moved from north-west London to the south-east, on the other side of the river, where I feel more connection with nature in a quieter environment. I moved here to mark the start of a new cycle and to be nearer to my job, which I lost two months later due to Covid-19. The loss was an opportunity to focus on what was most important to me, and to practice being instead of doing. It has been a roller coaster and still is. My mind and my body are sometimes on different paths but I have learnt that I am okay like this. Each small step is a success. Every day is a new beginning and I trust the seeds I have planted to grow so that my projects will become reality.

I am now thankful for every new day and the 24 hours that I can fill with new experiences. I would have never been able to find my way without amazing women, therapists, coaches, mentors and my support network. Each time I needed them, they were present to support me, highlighting where I have come from and what I have achieved so far. I tried a lot of techniques that were new to me and I had a lot of good, and less good, experiences that helped me become who I am.

I successfully freed myself from the real brace and also from the brace I had created in my mind. I still have a lot of resistance and contradictions but I accept them as part of myself and being human. I am alive and this is what matters.

Little Ballet Girl

By Christine Hale

Little Ballet Girl

*"My inspiration is to enable even those with
a life-limiting condition to live their best life."*

*I am standing in the middle of a large church hall in my freshly
washed pale blue leotard, flesh-coloured ballet tights and ballet shoes
with neatly tied ribbons. Everything is in place; even my hair is in a
regulation headband and net. I look ready for my primary-grade ballet exam at age six. Except I don't feel ready. I'm the only dancer on
the floor. The examiner behind the table and the pianist in a corner
are both strangers to me. I hold myself strong, even though inside I
am quaking. I do the barre exercises, point my toes, do my character
dance for all I am worth, and clap the rhythms of crotchets, minims,
and quavers successfully, despite my fears and sense of loneliness. My
parents didn't come, they never do – they are always busy with my
sisters and brother – but I pass the exam with "Commended" and
they are as happy at the news as I am.*

I learned a lot through my ballet classes: resilience, how to be
a pretend extrovert in order to divert attention, and that I could
protect myself with a self-created barrier. I carried on until I was
16, doing another six grade exams, my resilience growing even
stronger each year. I still love ballet to this day. I watch the Royal

Ballet when I can and I admire the strength, control, dedication, resilience and passion of the dancers. I have lived my life with this inspiration.

What is normal?

My life, until I was 54, was a "normal" life. My childhood had its usual ups and downs; I was one of four siblings – elder brother, elder sister, me and younger sister – and I was very much the "middle" child. My elder sister was diagnosed with scoliosis of the spine at 14 and my younger sister was born with mild cerebral palsy, so consequently both received a lot of attention. My ballet classes continued throughout my early years, as my parents felt I needed something that was "just for me." We had a happy family life, but my parents had some underlying stress, mainly driven by money, I think.

My teenage years were quiet, without loads of friends, boy-friends or girlfriends coming through the house as you might expect with four of us. We went to school in a town distant from where we lived, so our friends were spread far and wide. My college years were fun but I feel now that it was the wrong decision to go, as the qualification, a three-year diploma from a school away from home in Sheffield, did not assist me much in getting a job after leaving. Looking back, it was something I did because it was thought my grades wouldn't be good enough to get a place to train as a physical education teacher, a choice I often regret.

I am standing at the top of a ridiculously small "big" slope, skis on but not moving. I have been working as an au pair and the mum and I came to ski. After starting off together, she left me behind, racing to the bottom after seeing I was okay. I'm not sure how okay I could be as I have only skied once before. When low clouds rolled in, I was hardly able to see 50 metres ahead. Scared but insistent, I push myself, little by little, forward from the top of the slope, trailing other skiers until I reach the bottom. Little Ballet Girl has again found the courage to move forward despite her quaking.

I took my first ever flight just after leaving college, to work for nine months as an au pair and housekeeper in a lovely small French town, Ferney Voltaire. I have called this the best time in my life. I had been working a full-time pub job after college, as no career-forming opportunities were appearing. The opportunity to live abroad sounded enticing. My charge, Laurent, was 11 years old and an easy child to care for apart from his untidy bedroom. The mum, Hilary, worked, and the dad, Bob, was retired.

From the first minute in my new "home," I knew I had made a great decision. I was free, to a point, but much freer of mind and spirit than I had ever been at home. I enjoyed getting up early to go to the boulangerie every morning for baguettes and croissants. I loved my time there. I had a turquoise, left-hand drive Mini, I skied most weekends in a chic Haute Savoie resort, I earned good money for an au pair, massively improved my French and quite simply discovered myself for the first time. I was free of the expectations of others, which I always took to heart, and I was very, very, happy. I made lots of friends: other au pairs, German guys working at the Intercontinental Hotel, Americans working at the US mission/embassy and, of course, locals. My horizons broadened massively. I even went on a three-week holiday to the United States with the family, so my second-ever flight was on a jumbo jet.

When it was coming to the end of my time working for the family, I thought long and hard about staying in France but made the decision to return to England, responding to the family expectation to get a full-time job using my qualification. With that, I regret to say that my life really did become more "normal."

I met my husband when I was 30, having not had many boy-friends. We started off fun and adventurous, like all couples, but after some time I realised that too often I had to fit in with *his* family or friends. I did the organising for holidays and anniver-sary dinners. I did the shopping, cooked dinner and generally kept us going as the main earner in our marriage. This allowed my husband to do his own thing and run his own business, though he never made good money. We had a regular social life and went on some great holidays and adventures, but in truth they only served to fill the space that was growing between us. I decided to walk away after 20 years. I was tired of the rut, the lack of attention and support, and my own slow disappearance.

I left in 2008, just a year after my mother died. My father died in 1999, and I see now that perhaps I stayed in my marriage because I hadn't wanted my parents to see I had failed. Little Ballet Girl's resilience had held me steadfast, perhaps wrongly this time.

Working with heart
I spent 30 years working in the food flavouring business, which is an integral part of the food and drink manufacturing indus-try. In 2010, I was diagnosed with a stress-related illness caused by my job. An inattentive boss and lack of support in the hard-driven industry were affecting me both physically and mentally. I earned a great salary but I was never able to get a true foothold in the male-dominated environment. My clients liked me, my salary increased, but something was off.

I spent two weeks in a Priory Hospital. There I learned more about myself through mindfulness and Cognitive Behavioural Therapy. I faced my low self-esteem issues and did my first-ever yoga class on the hospital lawn. Under a huge oak tree with the sun shining down on me, a calm came over my mind and body. It felt glorious and I knew then that yoga was for me.

I returned to work certain that I had banished my gremlins. I had advanced on a potentially massive contract with a major client when, out of the blue, my company lodged a disciplinary procedure against me. I still to this day have no idea what caused them to take the action - it was unbelievable to me and to my colleagues. I felt a blow to the self-esteem that I had so carefully built up since my diagnosis, and decided I should leave for the sake of my mental health, but not on their terms. Somehow, Little Ballet Girl took charge again. I marched into my boss's office just before leaving to go home and said, "It is obvious you want me to leave, so I'm going, but you are going to pay!" With that, I turned and walked out of the door.

After two belittling disciplinary meetings at which they struggled to find any words to prove their case, with the help of a great employment lawyer I left with an appropriate settlement. It felt sweet to learn later that the account I had been working so hard on had come through and the client had told my former boss that I had been an important reason for their decision.

Reflecting on 30 years of working life, I realise that it was a rut I fell into, a "comfort zone" similar to the one I had experienced in my marriage. I was so blinkered into having a well-paid job that I didn't realise I was pushing myself toward a limit. When I finally had enough of being made to feel small, Little Ballet Girl again gave me the strength to walk away.

It was in December 2011 that my life really changed. I had been short of breath and easily fatigued for several months and finally went to my doctor to check it out. He immediately assigned me an appointment at the rapid-access heart clinic, where I was diagnosed with a genetic heart condition called hypertrophic cardiomyopathy. I had been fit and well all my life – skied many runs, scuba-dived, cycled up hills, run three half-marathons and climbed mountains. The diagnosis seemed impossible. I was analysed and thoroughly tested, though such was the abnormal rhythm of my heart that the treadmill test could have given me a stroke, so we left that one out. I left the clinic with my first collection of tablets, in a state of shock and unnerved by the diagnosis.

My heart journey had begun. I had gone to the appointment by myself, but Little Ballet Girl was there, standing tall and strong. She also sat with me on my sofa that night, wondering how all this could be, as I called my siblings to tell them my devastating news.

In the years since, I have had five ablations – an operation where they insert catheters inside your heart to attempt to stop unusual rhythms. Each of these lasted about five hours and involved three catheters being passed up a major vein into my heart – one a camera, another a guide and the third an electrical probe to burn the parts of my heart that were creating the abnormal rhythms.

Cath labs are not like normal operating theatres. They are full of equipment and people. I arrive into the lab on foot and climb onto the table where the procedure will be done under X-ray. There are at least 16 people there. A number of leads, wires and pads are attached to my body. It's always so cold. To one side are four massive screens to monitor the catheters' progress and position during the procedure. There is an anaesthetist who will keep me safely under general anaesthetic for more than five hours, plus nurses and at least six people in the annex room watching everything on screens. 'I always wanted to be on screen,' I tell them, 'but not this type, and not so many!' I listen to the consultant run through the checks and the planned procedure. Through all of this I experience a surprising level of calm, trusting that all will be right in the end. Then suddenly I'm out.

After each procedure my initial results were great and I had renewed energy, but gradually my heart returned to uneven rhythms. I faced these operations by myself, but friends would take me to hospital and see me settled. I set up a group text to family and friends to let them know I was still alive afterwards. It is strange, the feeling of waking up on your own after such invasive surgery and not having someone to hold your hand and tell you that you are okay. However, my friends would collect me after the procedure and look after me for a couple of days. My resilience carried me through and my courage stopped me getting lost in self-pity. Five times I went through this and five times I left the hospital smiling, thanks to Little Ballet Girl.

Fortunately, during this time I learnt to meditate and a friend introduced me to Reiki. I signed up for her course not knowing what to expect, but found that energy flowed easily through me when giving a treatment. The course opened my mind to spiritual learning, self-awareness and wellbeing. With this new set of tools to enhance my self-knowledge, I found a new place to "be" and an inner calmness that was visible to others. If this had not happened, I certainly would have struggled with all that was to come my way in the following years.

Transplanting my fears

Seven years into my heart journey came the greatest test of my life. I became aware in June 2018 that I was getting breathless and fatigued more easily. I went through a few tests and was called back to my cardiologist's clinic. My heart condition had deteriorated to the point that he said, 'I'm referring you for a heart transplant assessment.' Tears ran down my face. 'We always knew that this may happen,' he told me, allowing me to recover my poise before running through what the procedure would entail. Throughout all my time with him and my many appointments, urgent phone calls and operations, he has always been open and honest with me. This gave me confidence to face the challenge ahead, knowing that it was surely the right step. As always, at the end of my appointment, I hugged him. I was at the appointment by myself, so again left the hospital with conflicting emotions of dismay and hope. Potentially I would have a new heart that would allow me to live out the rest of my life and get back to the things I loved doing. I doubled up my meditation and self-awareness to create a deeper level of protection for myself. What was it going to be like, this procedure to put a new heart in my body?

I faced all the assessments with courage and a smile. I have a picture of me, dressed in my hospital gown, proudly showing off my two patient wristbands with a silly grin on my face. I lived in hope that this new heart would be the light at the end of the grey tunnel I had been living in. But that light was snuffed out after two key tests proved that I was not viable for transplant. My wail was loud and painful. Disbelief, loss, shock – countless emotions – and those tears again. My friend, Sam, stayed with me through that first night.

Fear engulfed me. What was available to help keep me alive, if not a transplant? Two technically advanced mechanical options were presented as possibilities, but were eventually disregarded as they would be debilitating and were essentially just support steps towards transplant. So, what next? A new medication was available. It was not specifically known for use with my type of cardiomyopathy, but my cardiologist was up for trying it out and so was I. At the same time as the transplant assessment, I had another procedure to go through…

I am under sedation at St. Peters Hospital to replace the "box" in my chest. I need a new one as the battery in my current box is running low. *The box is an Implantable Cardio Defibrillator and has three leads that are implanted in my heart. It paces my heart, controls fibrillation and will defibrillate my heart if it stops beating. It is an amazing piece of technology that keeps me alive and well. 'Hi everyone!' I say as I walk into the Cath Lab. Now I am lying on the operating table. Cold leads and pads are again attached to my body to monitor everything and read my box. Everything is in place to start the procedure. As I have only been sedated, I'm listening quite calmly to everything that is going on: the checks, the monitor readings that I am by now so accustomed to. The next thing I hear is the cardio technologist saying, 'Christine, we are turning off your ICD.' Suddenly I start to fight to get up. I'm sliding towards a bright light and I am frightened I am going to die. I am fighting with all my strength to get away. My arms and legs are flailing so much the nurses have to hold me down. Next, I hear a nurse's voice: 'Christine, Christine, it's okay, we've stopped the operation.' Fortunately, no incision had been made. They calm me down, reassure me I am okay, and to my great relief I am taken back to the ward. Two weeks later the procedure will be done successfully under general anaesthetic.*

The cumulative effect of these experiences gave me a level of Post-Traumatic Stress Disorder, not clinically diagnosed, but I know myself well. My anxiety was off the charts. The psychologist at Harefield Hospital identified this while I was at a review appointment. Fortunately, she and the palliative care team set me on a route to get support from a local hospice. This was a scary thought. Aren't they places where people go to die?

The support I received was wonderful. The counsellors and the wellbeing team encouraged me to set a new direction in my life, rebooting the positivity and inspiration that everyone else saw in me but seemed to have slipped from my grasp. Again, meditation, self-love and a deep learning of myself were key elements in finding and maintaining my balance. One of my friends once said to me, 'You have so much hope in you, such inner strength, a rod of iron!' It seems Little Ballet Girl always shone through. My brightness had dimmed a little, but my courage pushed me to step up and show how big and beautiful life can be, even with "end-stage heart failure." No one believes it, as I look a picture of health, but that is a question of mind over matter and a real self-knowing in all that I do. My heart shines, even if it is broken.

Inspiring others to live their best life

My unknown, unexpected, inherited heart condition diagnosis came from out of the blue. Previously, I thought a hamstring injury was a big deal! I could have fallen into a deep void of depression and self-pity, but instead, I experienced a light that I wasn't aware of until my heart condition was diagnosed. One of my favourite quotes is from the 13th century Persian poet, Rumi: 'The wound is where the Light enters you.'

Little Ballet Girl's resilience has given me a strong, positive attitude toward life, ever since I was six. I am aware of my condition but also of my general wellbeing. I have learned that meditation works for me and now I want to inspire people to find their truest self. Knowing that I can balance myself and find peace gives me a solid place to stand in this world, or I should say in 'my world,' as that is what is most important to me these days. I have learned to let go of friends and family whose voices and hands want to hold me back, in order that I can be a beacon to others rather than dimming my light to fit into their world.

'Don't ever let anyone dull your sparkle. Not me, not you, not any cardiologist types, not no one! Your inner light shines non-stop even when you think it's not there, carry on sparkling' – this was written in a 60th birthday card from my dear friend, Suzanne.

When describing me, people have used words like "tenacity," "positive mindset," "willingness to grow." I would have shunned these words had I not become aware that I have indeed grown in to this space where I now firmly believe in myself. My inspiration is to enable everyone, even those with a life-limiting condition, to get out there and live their best life. Grasp what you have in front of you – imagine what could go right! For me, what went right was that I was not viable for transplant. The drug I was prescribed brought great improvement to my heart, and still does, without the physical or mental trauma of having a new heart put in my chest. When I tell people I have end-stage heart failure, people ask, 'what is the prognosis?' I tell them I am going to live the fullest life I can until I'm at least 80. This is me, and I am not going anywhere!

If anyone had told me that at the age of 62 that I would have a serious heart condition but be living my life in a calm, happy and balanced way, I would never have believed them. I have renewed energy and strength. I regularly swim and practice yoga. I am active and fulfilled. I have also had dramatic lows in my life, including long-term bulimia, but by learning to love myself and trust who I am, I overcame this as well.

Little Ballet Girl is still with me now as I live my life. I sit or stand in my ballet posture – with hands, as was ingrained in me during 12 years of classes and exams – and I am ready to face anything. I am thriving in my new space, which I have learned to hold and retreat to when my body and mind tell me to. Loving yourself for all that you are is the greatest love you can give. Let go of your limitations, allow yourself to be your truest self, find the "you" that's been within since the day you were born and have the courage to fly your banner. It is not ego, it's showing people who you are. Ego stems from a place of falseness or an attempt to fit into other people's impression of how you should be. I spent far too many years in that space. Let go of your fears and allow yourself to feel who you really are. Where you end up may surprise you. Find your purpose; 'people without purpose perish' (Proverbs 29:18) as they have nothing to drive them forward.

I know that I have the integrity to hold my new-found form. I sometimes wish that I had known myself like this at least 20 years ago. My life would have been vastly different. But then I might not have found my inner space as clearly as I have. I could still be struggling with that former self. I am glad that I learned to break through my self-imposed barriers and have a fantastic 20-plus years to be "me". This is me, and I'm not walking away. I plan to carry on inspiring people to shine brightly from their heart and enjoy the infinite potential in their lives.

Little Ballet Girl has pirouetted and danced throughout my life and has now grown into a prima ballerina with grace, love, joy and sparkle in her heart. I am glad that young girl stepped up for her primary ballet exam. She has been with me all my life and will remain so. I can't fit into the swan tutu my mother made for me when I was eight, but it hangs in my bedroom along with a pair of ballet shoes to this day. Thank you for being there, Little Ballet Girl, and bringing resilience into my life. We shall keep dancing 'til the end of love.

SPIRITED
EMBRACING LIFE'S RICHNESS
FEARLESS
open
tolerance
blessed
DEEP
CURIOUS
INTREPID
adventurous
creative
TRUTHFUL

Learn to be a Chameleon

By Anja Loetscher

Learn to be a Chameleon

"I found out what inspires me,
discovered my talents and asked myself,
'what stands in the way of my dreams?'"

*T*o my mum: Mother, you made me who I am today. I would love for you to see how I live now in your home. You knew that I would end up living here – I never believed you.

Thank you for always supporting me. It must have been very diffi-cult for you at times when I was wandering around the world. Only now do I understand how you must have felt not having your family around. Sorry.

And you know what, Mother? It is only now, at age 66, that I realise I am a copy of you. You married an Ethiopian. How brave was that in 1955? Your family never spoke to you again. What we can learn from this is to follow what our heart says. Too often we listen to our mind instead of our intuition.

I married a Swiss – not as exotic as you – and started travelling the world with him. Africa was your home; Asia was mine. You travelled all over in your married life and loved to discover coun-tries on your own. In fact, you were one of the few women to travel through China alone, starting in Beijing, and ended up in Hong Kong, where I lived. You also met the most fascinating personalities *in your life: Haile Selassie, the Shah of Persia, the former King of Sikkim, William Tubman, former president of Liberia, and President Julius Nyerere from Tanzania, to name just a few.*

You had three children. Unfortunately both Endreas and Aida passed away, and now I am left. I had three children, too. Two were aborted, one was born in 1982; a fabulous daughter living now in the UK with two lovely children and an Italian husband. It seems we are continuing the habit of not marrying our own nationality.

You divorced at 40, moved to Germany and started all over again. I divorced at 40, moved to Germany and also started all over again. We were – and are – both very strong ladies. We do it our way. Though, we should have spent more time together over a glass of whiskey.

A couple of years back I attended a retreat in India, and at a meditation class, we were asked to draw or paint our life. I sat there for two hours not knowing what to draw. Suddenly I realised that my life seemed like a series of 20-year chunks. I drew a map of the continents and added names to them: 20 years in Africa, *Authenticity*; 20 years in Asia, Polynesia and Australia, *Adaptability*; 20 years in Europe and my career, *Faith*; my life now, *Gratitude*.

I have lived in more than 15 countries over the last 60-plus years and have experienced so many different things. It would take a whole book to cover just a fragment, but here I will share some major events and lessons I learned over each 20-year period. I am very grateful to have had the life I have lived so far, and the opportunity to learn so much in so many places. This has made "Anja" – who I am today.

One thing I should admit is that I do not recall everything anymore. Friends say, 'Anja, do you remember?' And I sometimes do not. I did go to see a doctor, who told me that it is quite normal, as I have seen so much and lived in so many places. Of course I cannot remember everything!

I have often been asked, 'Anja, where are your roots?' I have no roots. 'Anja, where did you like it best?' I loved everywhere I went. 'Anja, where is home for you?' Home is where I live now. I call myself a professional wanderer. I'm not even sure yet if Munich, where I live now, is my final destination.

Authenticity: 20 years in Africa

I started travelling at a year and a half, and I have never stopped. I was that age when my mum divorced my father and followed her first love, whom she had met in London, to Africa. We arrived in Nairobi on a freighter in 1955. How courageous was that? Leaving her husband and going with me to Africa to marry a black man.

I grew up in a "black and white" family, speaking English and Amharic at home. My dad was the Ambassador for Ethiopia and hence we moved around a lot. My mother told me that when she used to sit next to my dad in their car in Nairobi, the police would stop them and tell my mother that she was not allowed to sit next to her driver – it was her husband. When my brother was born in 1957, my father needed special permission to enter the "white" hospital to see his wife and his newborn son. What a change from Germany it must have been for my mother.

Once we started going to kindergarten, I could not understand why the children in school used to call my brother all kinds of names because of his colour when his name was Endreas. Not all the children had the opportunity to grow up in a mixed family. I was lucky, whether black or white, it did not matter to me – for me it was the most natural thing. This was the foundation for my future life. I never questioned colour, after all we are all human beings.

My sister, Aida, was born in Addis Ababa a couple of years later with a cleft lip and cleft palate. Little did I know what it would mean for her. She had to undergo operations every year until she died at the age of 21.

So, every summer my mother was gone with Aida for several weeks. We were allowed to buy pets from the road, and we had a ball. Once it was a monkey, then a sort of squirrel, but the best one was a crocodile. We transformed our bathroom into a jungle – the crocodile in the tub with some sand and plants all over so it felt at home. You can imagine the fit my mother had when she came home, and the tears we shed saying goodbye to our friend.

I was in English kindergarten and in German school later, and a lousy student in both. I barely finished high school. All I was interested in was skipping classes and going for motorbike rides with my boyfriend. So much for growing up on a fantastic continent.

What did I learn during 20 years in Africa? Authenticity. I had a carefree childhood. It did not matter what colour my friends were, we were all the same. I adapted to new countries and languages easily, which influenced the next phase of my life. I learned not to fear things and to "go for it." Though I was not good in school, it didn't influence my career in later life in the least.

Oh, I almost forgot! My parents used to say that they would buy me a banana plantation. I used to sit on the roof of the Land Rover and eat bananas all day. Funny, I do not even like bananas anymore.

Adaptability: 20 years in Asia

I married a Swiss man working in the hotel industry in Dubai. I did not know at the time that this marriage would take me around the world. As with my dad, we were also posted in different countries. Bangkok, then a short stop in Switzerland to give birth to our daughter, then Bahrain, Hong Kong and Darwin, followed by Tahiti before going back to Hong Kong and on to Dhaka, then back to Hong Kong again. Are you dizzy yet? A post in Istanbul was the last one with my husband. I enjoyed every minute of our life – new countries, new continents, new languages and different spices. I could go on and on. Sometimes we stayed for two years, sometimes for four, but always with enough time to get to know the place.

We always lived in hotels and didn't need to look for housing, but rather searched for schools for our daughter and doctors in case of need. Our top priority was to meet the local people. We didn't especially look to mingle with people from our home countries.

One thing I perfected through all these moves was packing my suitcase. These days, I only have to start a half-hour before I leave for a trip!

Being the wife of a General Manager in a hotel has advantages and disadvantages. Suddenly you have many "friends," but these are often people who want to take advantage of getting a free meal or a day at the pool. For our daughter, we needed to be sure that she wasn't spoiled by the attentive staff. She also had many "friends" wanting to swim or have an ice cream. Living in hotels felt like being on stage all the time. Everyone knew when we left and when we came back. To make a hotel room feel more like home, I always transformed the bathroom in our suite to include a kitchen. It meant so much just to eat a homemade fried egg once in a while.

I can't deny enjoying the luxury of having a cook, a driver and a 24-hour nanny, but there are always two sides to the coin. I did not want to sit at the pool and have drinks all day, every day, so I decided to take up jobs wherever we lived. I did not have to have a career of my own. It was not about money, but rather about learning new things.

In Dubai, I worked as a ticketing agent for Japan Air Lines. In Bangkok, I took up Ikebana, Japanese flower arranging, when I was unable to get a work permit. In Bahrain, I was responsible for all the Benetton boutiques, which was my first time selling clothes in a boutique.

Over the years in Hong Kong, I had different jobs. Never having worked in the import business before, I imported garments from India – I love India, I must have been Indian in my former life. I trained Ikebana teachers and imported Laura Secord chocolates – this must have been my Swiss side, though the chocolate came from Canada.

In Darwin, again without a working permit, I started to learn to fly a Cessna. This was really new.

'Anja, the next round you fly on your own.'

The day had come for my first flight without my teacher. I took off and did my round, and the tower was broadcasting all kinds of instructions but I did not pay attention, I was so focused on coming down again in one piece.

'Anja do you have a biro?' I was asked. 'Please take down the following number and contact us once you have parked the plane.'

I had created major chaos at Darwin Airport by not following instructions. I really caught it from them. Nevertheless, I received my license and continued to fly in Hong Kong. For those of you who knew the old airport, it was an adventure to land between two jumbo jets on the only runway. Here, a saying from Africa comes to my mind: "If you think you are too small to make a difference, you haven't spent a night with a mosquito." I felt like that mosquito.

After Darwin, we were assigned to Tahiti, a dream land of blue, crystal-clear water and lovely music. I still hear it and picture the beautiful beaches, and the one road around the island. Here I ventured into creating a book on how to tie pareos – my first time writing a book, before contributing to this compilation of wise women's words.

As you can see, I never tolerated a dull moment. I embraced all situations, invented new ones, and made the best out of all that crossed my path.

Unfortunately, we did not stay in Papeete for long before we left for Dhaka, a "hardship destination." Here there was poverty and corruption, no shops to buy food, and the nearest hospital was in Bangkok. Again without a working permit, I became a Brownie leader at my daughter's school. I enjoyed it so much and I think my love for children's yoga, which I currently teach, had its roots there, my grandsons having given me the final push to go ahead with this.

From Dhaka, we went back to Hong Kong and were scheduled to go to Bali for our next assignment. We flew there, checked out schools and came back to pack.

'Anja, what are all these boxes in the corridor?' asked Phyliss, a friend and well-known clairvoyant.

'We are leaving for Bali,' I replied.

'No, you are not.'

'What do you mean we are not? We found a school and we will be living in the hotel. It's a beautiful place.'

'You will be going to a place with lots of church towers, not to Bali,' she told me.

The next day, we were reassigned from Bali. We waited six full months before we learned of our next station: Istanbul, a place with lots of church towers!

What did I learn during 20 years in Asia? Adaptability. There were so many opportunities, I just needed to find them and take time to meet and integrate into the local communities, to learn new languages and skills, and not forget the culinary discoveries in every country. I learned to enjoy what life has to offer – and to be open to it.

Faith: 20 years in Europe

In Istanbul, I started the beginning of a new life and the end of my married life. I had wanted to leave the artificial hotel world I lived in, but never found the right time or place for divorce. One evening I got out of bed in Istanbul, called our driver, left the hotel and never turned back. I was divorced within two days.

I had a heavy knot in my chest for a very long time and it would not go away; a dark tunnel from not knowing whether to stay in Istanbul or move somewhere else. What about schooling for my daughter and work for me? I had not needed to work to earn money, but now the coin flipped, and I needed to start earning a living to survive.

I decided to go to Germany. I found a job within two days in Munich, working at the reception desk for a hotel group. I found a flat within a week, within walking distance of school and my job. My daughter had been going to American schools and she spoke German, but could not read and write it. I found a student in a higher-grade class to tutor her on homework at our home, while I was working.

Both of us had to adapt to a new way of living, with no friends and little money to live on. Of course, we survived. My daughter graduated with straight As – not like me. We flourished. I climbed the career ladder, year after year. All my jobs came to me – I never applied for one – and now, in retirement, I'm still as active as ever. No more knot in the chest and no more dark tunnel. I continued always to further my education. During every holiday, I spent some time learning something new, something that had nothing to do with my job. It was so enriching, just like all those years that I spent with Ikebana, chocolate and planes.

The world has so much to offer. Find out what inspires you, discover your talents and ask yourself what may be standing in the way of you accomplishing your dreams. "Curiosity" and "lifelong learning" are words that define my life.

What did I learn over 20 years in Europe? Faith. I learned to believe in myself, to have courage and to eliminate fear. The "how" came as I went forward.

Gratitude: My life now

Thank you to all who stood next to me in challenging times. Thank you for supporting all my crazy ideas. Thank you all for your trust. Today, I fly to save lives, transporting bone marrow and stem cells for cancer patients. I teach yoga classes for adults and children – do come by if you live in Munich! I study neurographics, a discipline invented by Russian psychologist Pavel Piskarev in 2014. Neurographics compromises two words: neuron, a cell that carries messages between the brain and other parts of the body; and graphics, the artistic use of pictures, shapes and words. It is a tool to help you achieve your goals through drawing. Now I can draw my life!

I take a group each year to Pondicherry in India. I monitor student examinations twice a year at the hotel management school in Geneva. I still want to get myself a motorbike, though I'm not sure if it is sensible at the age of 66. Maybe I should start with a scooter first?

In the time I have left, I will see family and friends all over the world. Recalling my regret for not spending enough time with my mother, I want to spend as much time as possible with my daughter and family.

I found out what inspires me, discovered my talents and asked myself, 'what stands in the way of my dreams?'

Thank you, Mother, for everything.

My Luxury Life
Was My Prison

By Claudia Roth

My Luxury Life Was My Prison

"Only after a thorough dismantling could I stand back up with new awareness and reassemble the pieces to connect to a new part of myself."

The first time I knew for sure that something was not quite right was when I woke up in a luxury suite at the Ritz in Paris. Early morning sunshine illuminated the white marble bathroom and I gazed into a mirror as wide as two oversized sinks, only to see a giant Blackberry imprint checkerboarded on my cheek. My work was literally disfiguring me.

As I look back on the transition from being a high-flying corporate executive to a simple "no one" riding her scooter in Auroville, a spiritual community in the south of India, I conclude that my search was always for freedom. Only, I was looking for it in all the wrong places.

Choosing the road less travelled is not easy. The path takes sharp turns into the undergrowth, only to disappear suddenly: it doesn't present itself clearly, nor does it seem promising, and that is precisely the point. Every step will always be a leap into the void, but that is where freedom hides in plain view, ready to surprise.

Conditioned beliefs are a global pandemic

My grandmother had an important influence on me as I grew up in a small town in Germany. A confident and resourceful woman, her hands carried marks from working hard in the field picking potatoes. She created a sense of comfort, given her warm and slightly oversized nature. She was also a business woman who had lived through the First and Second World Wars, and she instilled in me the ethic, "work hard, be successful and you can have everything in life." My mother, my father and most people around me were of the same opinion and I embarked on this same path without much questioning.

In my 20s, I was settled in London and busy creating a place for myself in the world of luxury hospitality. One small but vivid memory from when I began my corporate climb, which seemed inconsequential at the time, foretold a curiosity that would take me places. I was sitting on a red, double-decker bus moving through busy traffic. It was a sunny spring morning and I was excited, on my way to the office, my first proper workplace. Observing people boarding and alighting the bus, as if they had done it for years, I realised how we all live such different lives. I was intrigued by these differences and there, on that noisy bus, I had a fleeting insight into what would become my role as a curious traveller, through landscapes both inside and out.

I was relentless in my pursuit. Early on, selling luxury cruise trips, I travelled to China and felt energised to be in a place so different. Suddenly part of a bus convoy following police cars that cleared the streets, we were able to make our way effortlessly through traffic that was made up not of cars but of what seemed like millions of cyclists. Were they all going to work, like me?

The harder I worked the better, and I was afforded unimaginable perks – dinners in Michelin-starred restaurants, meeting prominent people like His Holiness the Dalai Lama, experiencing so many famous sites around the world. Then, in 1999, in Frankfurt, I was driving home after yet another late night at the office when something strange happened.

It flies at me out of nowhere; a large car lunges into my beloved BMW and my forehead slams into the hard plastic of the steering wheel. The next thing I'm aware of is being wheeled on a stretcher. Two white-clad men are preparing to lift me, stretcher and all, into an ambulance. When I am inside, my friend Harald mysteriously appears by my side, but rather than show gratitude I grab his scarf and pull him close. 'Harald, I have an important meeting tomorrow. I don't have time for this,' I tell him, waving my arms around. 'I have stuff to do. How is my car?'

'You always have an important meeting, Claudia,' he replies. 'Rush, rush, rush...'

Realising that the ambulance is about to move, I shriek. 'My laptop, my phone!' Not until my Fendi bag is by my side, laptop and phone safe inside, do I rest my head back on the pillow. The ambulance doors close.

The hospital emergency ward reeks of antiseptic as a doctor presses my limbs here and there. I tell him I feel fine, but to my horror, I'm not immediately released. I am given a room to wait for the doctor's decision. Harald sits down by my side clutching a cup of coffee.

'Do you want some?'

'No, thank you, dear Harald. I want to call Willie.'

Willie is my husband. I bite distractedly on a chipped red nail that has broken off. 'The sheets are synthetic,' I add.

The next day, I wasn't able to move but neither the doctors nor the chiropractor found a single thing wrong with my bones and joints. It became clear that there was something else going on. The chiropractor gave me a prescription for massages and it turned out that the masseuse was a healer in disguise. He got me back on my feet, working with energies and the subtle physical. I started to realign myself. Clearly my mind had been holding me back: some fear I harboured had caused my immobility, rather than any physical injury.

Did this sudden and surprising realisation help me venture deeper into explorations of how my mind was affecting me? No. I got on with the work at hand. On the surface, I was fully involved with the luxury life, but beneath it the feeling that there was more to life than the material was growing and causing me some degree of unease.

Fear of flying couldn't keep me down

I regularly criss-crossed the globe, as the head office I was working for was based in New York. I didn't feel exhaustion from this mobile career, not from the constant long hauls and not from the long hours at work. I was intoxicated with my lifestyle and my success but there were issues bubbling up to disturb me. A budding fear of flying conspired to slow me down, but I resisted. I insisted on flying, even though I was terrified. As I felt my heart fall out of my chest while boarding yet another plane, I understood it was irrational but I had nothing to hold onto up in the air. I couldn't even hold on to myself. I was in a free-fall but still I brushed off as madness any thought of changing my career.

Today seems as good a day as any for a plane to crash at take off. I have imagined so many crashes. Although I consider staying in the Business Lounge forever, I board the plane. Just after take-off, I open my laptop and type a resignation letter. I don't mean a word of it; I am just tricking my mind to stay calm for a little bit longer.

'It's crazy,' I hiss to myself as I type. The woman sitting next to me in the aisle seat looks at me, then she looks away. 'S**t,' I think, 'I've

*lost it'. Buckle up, Claudia! My seat belt is already fastened, of course,
not that it makes me feel any safer. I doubt I know what to do in an
emergency. What if I can't remember? Will I die in the crash? I am
again gripped by a metallic fear of flying, but it's more than that. I
can't cope. I never want to board a plane again.*

*The flight attendant stops by my seat. She looks at me, her forehead
so scrunched that I see the cracks in her foundation. 'You're not well,'
she says.*

*'Of course I'm not well,' I snap back, panic raging inside. Despite
my attempt to appear strong – black travel power-outfit, pearl necklace, red nails – I am not.*

*'I'll send the pilot over to talk to you,' she says, giving me an
encouraging smile, then continues down the aisle. She must know
I'm not here to take a once-in-a-lifetime holiday flight.*

*Once we have taken off and the "fasten seatbelt" signs are no longer
on, the pilot squats next to me. Slightly on the larger side, he intro-
duces himself as Rick. Senior British Airways Captain Rick helps
keep me up in the air. He assures me that I am not being ridiculous
and tells me that many business people fear flying. 'They are used to
being in control,' he says.*

Later on I would have the chance to sit in a flight simulator
with Captain Rick, though it didn't cure my fear of flying. I was
on the ground, yet the simulated turbulence terrified me. I wasn't
in control. I wasn't, in that moment, "successful Claudia". The
illusion of turbulence caused a sense of vertigo in my self-image
that was horrifyingly real. Too many illusions; were we flying or
not? Was I successful Claudia or not? I just wanted to be back
on solid ground.

I knew I had to make a change, but "strong Claudia" whispered
in my ear, telling me I was doing just fine. I did not yet understand that keeping so busy had been a reaction to my insecurity.

My life was about proving myself. I needed outside validation to feel good and career success provided this, but was that freedom?

Free-falling... then grounded

Some hints toward change started to come my way. In 2005, I was in Delhi for work and took some time off to explore the south of India with my husband. A client set up a meeting for me in Pondicherry. True to form, I assumed that it would be a work meeting, but Vijaybhai Poddar spoke of completely different things. 'What is your purpose in life?' he asked, and as I answered with tired platitudes about work and success, I felt something stir deep inside. I was out of my depth, yet somehow aware that I might be only scratching the surface of my own potential. It turned out I was in discussion with a senior member of the Sri Aurobindo Ashram.

I began to ask myself if my focus on being a somebody, constantly projecting a "perfect image" of myself to the world, was a kind of virus that was actually weakening me? I was closer to believing that something must change.

I recall the imprint of the Blackberry on my cheek. At that point I wondered if my superficial lifestyle had become a trap that would scar me. Perhaps this was my point of no return? One evening at a business reception, every conversation seemed trivial. I detached from the role of being "strong Claudia, the high-flying executive" and a momentary sense of real freedom overcame me. I remembered my meeting at the ashram and an inner voice reminded me that there might be more to life than working hard to "be someone".

I realised that inner voice was me, too, and by hearing its calls for me to be still and pay attention, I was able to access ever more enlightening experiences, and stay in touch with myself. I continued asking questions, one of which was, 'Do I really have everything that I want?' Though it seemed so on the surface, if I was being honest with myself, I felt empty. All the Champagne and ocean views of the world could no longer fulfil me.

My inner voices played tug-of-war as my tangible, clear-cut professional world sparred with the intangible possibilities evoked by my new questions. After a painful battle, I quit.

I was suddenly at home with no office to go to, lost in self-reflection with an empty suitcase staring at me from one corner of my room. I imagined it feeling just as useless and deserted as I was. Nobody was asking for my expertise and I began to fear the onset of a completely unfamiliar depression.

I felt like I was free-falling and started to wish for the moment I would hit the ground, as I had in my imaginary plane crashes. At home and unwanted, this new victim version of myself that I had morphed into was even more painful than the terror of my imaginary crashes. Being unemployed was no accident. I had made it happen. It once made sense, and then it didn't.

My negative inner voices led me into some dark places. I felt myself disintegrate, disappear altogether. There were days when I could not get out of bed. I saw no meaning anywhere, in anything, anymore. I was no longer the successful corporate warrior that I had grown so attached to over more than two decades. I was so used to "doing" as opposed to "simply being". Though I had made it to the top, I felt I was still not good enough. I think that most high-achievers can identify with this if they are honest with themselves. It is a mainstream belief that "doing" and "achieving" matter more than "being".

Eventually, the new world called louder. A voice spoke up. "Get going, Claudia," it said. My conditioned self and my grandmother's voice came to my rescue and made sure I was putting in the work to recreate myself again.

A stranger in the forest holds up a mirror

I revisited the ashram in Pondicherry and also ventured into nearby Auroville. With a vague idea of writing a book about spirituality and business, I arranged a meeting with a man called Vijay. Braving mud tracks and puddles, I ventured into the forest.

I don't know this man, "Vijay without a phone," whom I am about to meet. He has answered my message in the Auroville community newsletter, and after exchanging a couple of emails we have arranged to meet. He has made it clear to me that he doesn't understand anything about luxury, but perhaps could help with my spiritual search.

I haven't told anyone where I'm going. Perhaps I should at least have informed the guest house I'm staying at, or Willie, but what can he do from London? I try to convince myself that it's the right thing for me to be here, right now. I love adventure, right?

Arumugam, the guest house taxi driver, parks next to a simple wooden sign with just a "P" for Parking. The paint is flaking off. I haven't asked Arumugam if he knows where Vijay's house is. He doesn't. We wander through the tall grass, looking for the right house and avoiding puddles as much as possible. There are probably snakes here as well, I think. There are no house numbers, of course. There are no street names, or even streets. No lights either.

Mud splashes up onto my white linen trousers and the humble heels of my shoes sink so far into the mud, I fear they'll get stuck. What was I thinking, dressing like this? With relief I spot a couple and ask them if they know Vijay's house. They smile and point, 'First one on the left, a blue one, just after the hibiscus bush.'

As we walk around the hibiscus, a Doberman jumps up and barks, and it occurs to me that despite my fear of flying or the trials of leaving my professional life behind, I am more scared right now than I've ever been in my entire life. Just then I hear a distant but cheerful, 'Claudia, willkommen!' He sounds German, or maybe Italian.

Vijay walks towards us, his hair greyish-white, eyes squinting.

I clutch the mobile phone with its temporary Indian number. Holding it close to my chest, I regret wearing the necklace almost as much as I regret the white trousers. I feel totally out of place. At least I have a phone, out here in the middle of nowhere. I check the signal. There is no signal. But then, who would I call if there were a signal?

'Give me your number,' I tell Arumugam. Just in case. 'Better safe than sorry,' I can almost hear my grandmother mutter.

I offer Vijay my hand. 'Om,' he says, placing his joined palms in front of his chest. Luckily, I am aware that the joined palms in front of Vijay's chest mean "I greet the Divine in you" and is common in India. Instinctively I mirror it, which saves me from looking very silly with one hand stretched out in mid-air.

He has a soft but manly voice, definitely Italian, I note as we introduce ourselves. He's not wearing western clothes, but instead a kind of hippyish kurta – a loose shirt without a collar – and plain cotton trousers. He greets Arumugam, then turns back.

'Come with me,' he says. I follow him towards the house, indicating to Arumugam to wait nearby.

We're in the middle of a lush forest garden. A porch runs along the front of the house and seemingly all around it. The house is made of bricks, painted blue. It seems at peace with the surrounding trees. The windows are made of steel mesh to let the breeze through while keeping mosquitoes out. In front of the house, on the ground, all sorts of rocks, pebbles and crystals are laid out in a circular geometric pattern with a large white crystal at the centre.

'What's that?' I ask, having never seen anything like it.

'It's a mandala,' Vijay answers. 'It represents the universe.' At the door, he takes his shoes off and so do I. 'The rose quartz represents the heart chakra, which regulates our interactions with the external world and controls what we embrace and what we resist.'

I nod, understanding nothing, and follow him inside, wanting to leave the door ajar behind me in case I have to get out fast, but Vijay asks me to close it because of the mosquitoes, and so I do.

Vijay was born Vittorio Gresele in Italy, but the spiritual founder of Auroville, Mirra Alfassa, gave him the name Vijay. He asked me to tell him about myself and I rattled off my name, my past career, my vague thoughts of a new career, my husband… all that I figured encapsulated "me". He then held up a mirror before my face and asked, 'Is this who you are?'

This simple yet profound action suggested that I was living an illusory life, even though I was not yet able to grasp it. My ego had been desperately holding on to my much-pampered and proud idea of myself, but it was not that "Claudia" who stared back at me in Vijay's mirror. Who was I? I was catapulted out of what I can only call a deep sleep.

We have several images of ourselves that we keep polishing, developing various selves according to our upbringing, the expectations of different people and the situations we find ourselves in. Most of us are one person at home, one with friends – one image per set of friends perhaps – and one at work.

We are careful creatures of comfort. Had life not presented me with the road signs to lead me off the high-speed highway of corporate life, I might still be on it, as if in a self-driving car. I would neither have ventured into the wilderness of emptiness, nor have found that in that wilderness true freedom lurks.

Today I laugh at the surrealistic inner conflict, pitching my true self against my ego. The truth is that it is an on-going process, each battle won providing relief and a renewed sense of purpose.

Radical insights, gradual change
When I returned from India, I nurtured my interest in all things spiritual, but this brought new conflict. Nobody I knew was ask-

ing questions along the lines of "Who am I?" Nobody practiced meditation. Vijay had guided me towards many spiritual practices and I felt compelled to stick with them. To avoid losing connections, friends even, I hid this newly found passion.

I started my company, Soul Luxury, in an attempt to combine my old career experience with new learning. I persistently spent at least one hour every day connecting to myself. Awakened by my encounter with Vijay, it seemed clear that a force within would be available to me for my own rescue when I needed it. Much larger than myself and yet an intimate part of myself, it had always been there, just ignored.

I continued to hide my new interests, sure that nobody would understand me. After all, even I was wondering what I was getting myself into. Retreating to my room to meditate after business meetings felt like ducking out; what was it all for? Slowly, however, the "ego" of my fast-paced corporate life faded away as I sat with myself, discovering an altogether different "Claudia".

Everything is energy and everything shifts rather than disappears. So too, nothing is ever lost. Think about water. Whether in solid ice form, liquid, or gaseous vapour, the essence of it is always there. I started to see that perhaps all the effort that I put into my career in the past, my natural ability to persevere, focus and work hard, could come in handy in my new world. Able to see that I was not alone, I connected to people who were as "mad" as I was. Others, too, were looking for that elusive "something more" that is equally "something less," and understanding this helped. It helped to meet others also seeking higher truths and the accompanying purpose beyond leading a hollow life.

I focused on the negative impact of my former belief system to break free from it. Hard work can be both important and beneficial, but I was working to be accepted, moving in the most luxurious environments to feel special and validated. Surrendering and allowing myself to quit and fall down completely played an important part in my escape from this pattern that was keeping me imprisoned. Only after a thorough dismantling could I stand back up with new awareness and reassemble the pieces to connect to a new part of myself.

I emerged on the other side of the darkness. I persevered in my meditation and undertook many different explorations, attending sound-bath sessions and shamanic healing circles. I felt stronger, better, freer and more aware than ever before. The fog had lifted and I no longer cared what anyone might think about my new way. Only my inner compass mattered.

I have grown into a role combining "outer luxury" and "inner luxury", becoming a catalyst for change and transformation. As long as we recognise the joy and beauty of life hidden beneath our conditioning and self-images, the outer luxury doesn't rule us, rather it allows us to connect with the joy and beauty in us.

Life provides a stage for all kinds of magic. The more you believe it, the more you will receive, I have learned. If you find yourself at a dead end at work or in your personal life, when the point of no return appears, trust in the magic. This is the best springboard for taking the risk and jumping into the unknown.

These days I live in London and I'm letting my old life fade away, establishing myself in the new. I do think fondly of my globetrotting career and my adventurous experiences, but I know that I have changed. With less outer luxury and less travelling, there is freedom in following the inner voice. I was guided to explore my own stillness, experiencing it as a dynamic and nourishing space. If I look at who I was before and who I am now, the two women are miles apart. I have changed from the inside out. I found freedom inside myself, a space I have come to love and treasure. And so, the journey continues.

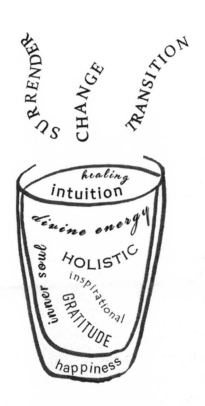

Transformation

By Astrid Salas

Transformation

*"Am I still struggling with uncertainty? You bet.
Childhood experiences do not vanish so simply, but I
learned that our bodies reflect our unspoken emotions."*

Have you ever wondered, "Why am I here? What is my mission?" When I ask myself these questions, I intuitively focus on the idea of "transformation". My story is related to the process of transition we all experience during our lives; that willingness to do a deep dive into yourself and discover your true calling. This process of transformation is not something you can determine by setting a date or a deadline; it may take years. I sometimes even wonder if there is ever an end to it. Are we not meant to continue developing ourselves mentally, physically and spiritually throughout our lives? Are we not continuously challenged to keep the balance of harmony between our body and our soul? Looking back to how I started and where I am today, my answer to these questions is "yes."

Childhood changes

When I was four years old, we moved from Colombia in South America to the Caribbean. This placed me in a new environment, interacting with strange kids speaking strange languages.

I remember feeling scared at the beginning. I felt insecure; an uncertainty that I believe has its roots in my traumatic start as a newborn. My pregnant mother was taken to the hospital by someone on the street. My father did not care about her pregnancy; he was too busy living his own life as a playboy. Through a lack of resources and ignorance, my mother was not prepared for my birth. It was a tough delivery but I was allowed to see the light of life. A guardian angel dressed as a nurse brought her some diapers and baby clothes, and after she was released from the hospital, she returned home with her baby girl in her arms.

By the time I started to feel at ease in kindergarten, it was time to move to primary school, which was located in another neighbourhood: new kids, new environment, another new beginning. Children are often expected to naturally adapt to the flow of changes caused by the decisions of their parents. Thinking back, these decisions made by my mother helped me to develop my ability to adapt quickly to new circumstances, and today I retain this flexibility, but an underlying feeling of uncertainty remained and also became part of me.

As adolescents we begin to realise our choice to protest or object to choices made by our parents. In adulthood, we are allowed and expected to create our own lives and also take responsibility for our own choices. My life has always been a journey of change. So, what is the difference between change and transformation? Change is about using external influences to modify actions to achieve desired results. Transformation is about modifying beliefs so that natural actions lead to the desired results. I didn't always know the difference. I am drawn to a beautiful quote from Reinhold Niebuhr: 'Change is the essence of life: Be willing to surrender what you are, for what you could become.'

The butterfly, a universal symbol of change, became my mascot. It began to show up for me everywhere: near my house or far from home in nature. I was fascinated by her variety of colours, and her company was confirmation that perhaps I should do something different or start something new. I was looking around me for what to change.

There was a moment when I sensed something different: something coming from deep inside, confirming my sense that I needed to change myself. This time it did not seem to come from my head – from thinking about my situation. I felt it was not about a career move or any of the changes I already knew and had experienced. It was different, yet I could not put a finger on it. All I knew was that it was coming from somewhere inside me.

Some people have experiences like this during silent walks in nature. I have a friend who finds guidance through inspirational cards. I like churches for their Divine energy. For other people it is their "gut feeling." Sometimes even a conversation can unleash something. My strong belief is that the message that is intended for you will get to you one way or another. If you do not catch it the first time, don't worry: the message is insistent.

I started to question myself: "What is wrong? Where is this feeling of discontent coming from?" I had everything my heart desired. Good health, a beautiful family, a nice house, great job, travel, great friends, a trendy car. Life was good. I didn't perceive yet that I was connected with my ego to the outer world. My need for change was coming from deep inside, from my inner soul. How was I supposed to know this? I was so busy with work; there was never time to connect to a soul. Actually, I was not even aware that I could connect to my body or soul.

As is often the case, while you are in your comfort zone it is not easy to make changes. Your own comfortable thoughts tell you to keep doing what you're doing. There are so many reasons to stay there. The mind is not always in harmony with the heart. Our brain is conditioned to perform according to what we think, say and believe. As Bobby Schuller, a well-known preacher in the United States, often says: 'Change your life, change your thoughts!' Never underestimate the power of the ego. It would have us believe that we have to keep up with or do better than others. Our ego listens to what the outer world says or expects from us, and we make this pattern part of our daily routine, measuring success by status and material belongings.

I can still hear my daughter, then nine years old, complaining, 'Mom, everybody at school has a Dolce Gabbana-na shirt except me,' mispronouncing the name of the designer in the sweetest way. It was Dolce & Gabbana, but it could have been an iPhone or Nike sneakers. Even at her tender age, this attention to brands was part of being something, being seen and appreciated for what you have instead of who you are. What does a nine-year-old girl really know about branding? Early on, the commercial world leads us to become material people, guided by smart marketeers to depend on external factors for identity. We forget that there will always be someone performing better, with more money and greater success.

It took perseverance and determination for me to understand the message from my inner voice. I was working hard to keep 100 balls juggling in the air, combining my hectic full-time job at a large international company with my many other responsibilities as a single mother. During that restless period of inner turmoil, I suffered from migraines, restless legs and sleeping disorders. I was reaching peak burn-out potential. I had burned out before, so the symptoms were familiar to me. I stopped seeing friends, I felt I was not grounded anymore, I felt lost.

Five sessions with a burn-out coach challenged me to recognise that I had bottled up anger and other destructive emotions; anger around childhood shortcomings, the absence of a father, an empty feeling of loneliness for not having had brothers or sisters. I used to cry out of earshot of my mother. I felt rejected and insecure. This uncertainty became a common thread within my emotional interactions, especially in relationships. I held on to a fear of abandonment. I also encountered anger as a result of not understanding myself. I was resistant to acknowledge that everything within me was crying for attention, for self-love and for change. I was so terribly afraid to jump into the unknown. I had a great job but I was very annoyed with the uncertainty of situations developing at work. I was in a lonely struggle with myself for survival.

The transition begins

At midday on September 13, 2015, I was told that my position had become redundant due to global reorganisations within the company. This partially explained my restlessness as a neglected hunch.

My father passed away that same evening. Although he was not actively present in my life, nor did he have any kind of meaningful contribution to my education, I feel we are always connected to our parents by the laws of nature. He passed away in the United States and I was in Amsterdam, but I was able to speak to him just hours before he died. I was able to express my sincere forgiveness that he was not the father I had needed.

That day hit me with a tsunami of emotions. I was filled with sadness for a double loss: disappointment at being made redundant after 21 years of loyalty and hard work for the company; anger and grief from the realisation that my father had lived such a miserable life and that I never found the right moment or the courage to tell him how he had harmed his abandoned child. Everything came together that day.

After finishing work, my focus suddenly turned inward to myself, rather than my job. By focusing on the love inside me, I started to see my daughter more clearly. I saw sorrow in her eyes and felt a most heart-breaking pain. I became more conscious of her needs and the challenges she was facing as a sensitive adolescent, and this began years of more open connection between us.

Coincidentally, although they say there is no such thing as coincidence, during that same period, a friend of mine, today an author, started to offer meditation classes in his attic. In those days, meditation and yoga were considered a bit floaty, at least in my circles. Nonetheless, I committed to join this little group in an attic doing "weird" things. It turned out to be an eye-opener for me. I learned that if you quieten yourself, you can actually hear your heart. I learned about the presence of chakras and meridians in our bodies, about visualisation and affirmations. Silence became my best friend. I stopped talking all the time in order to become a better listener.

Half a year later, much earlier than I had envisioned, I accepted a managerial position once again. I was charged with the introduction of a new airline into the marketplace. No small task, but I accomplished this and several other commercial roles, conscious that I was deviating from my path of transformation and falling again into stressful jobs.

I noticed that despite all the stress I worked with my clients as people rather than focusing solely on their business objectives. I fulfilled my role from a counsellor's perspective, rather than as a commercial professional. I was connecting differently. Although I was never a good reader before, I was now attracted by articles and books about personal development and spirituality. I was eager to learn how to make a better version of myself by having more self-belief and understanding the incredible influence of emotional intelligence. My psychological sensors were activated.

Once I started to refocus, I attracted people similar to the "new me," without particularly seeking them out. I found myself meeting others who were also searching for their purpose in life. I had more in-depth conversations than ever before about myself, and at the same time I was fascinated to listen to what others had to say about themselves. Some of my old friends were still around but our conversations were different. I was prepared to recognise that, as I evolved spiritually, not everyone would stay close and some people's journey on the train of my life may come to an end. I learned to release the disappointment I felt that our paths had developed differently. I understood that everyone follows their own track and that new friends would come on board to contribute to my journey. The most wonderful new passengers were getting on board the train I was now on.

I also experienced moments of fear and that old, questioning uncertainty, "What if I am wrong? What if my new world isn't as rewarding? Will I be happy? Will I feel at ease?" This doubt made it difficult for me to stay focused on this new road that I was trying to follow.

For a person who has spent most of her life feeling insecure, choosing a next step is scary. I finally made that step when I realised that I had a choice. I could go back to the old world and continue a career-oriented life, or I could choose to continue my search for inner calm, following my heart and believing in myself. I immersed myself in self-reflection, and the more I talked about it with the new people in my life, the more convinced I became that I was not going back. My previous world was dominated by ego, driven mainly by thoughts, stressful jobs, a hurried life and multitasking to accomplish goals. It represented a lack of balance between body, soul and spirit. I became convinced that it was not the right match for me anymore.

I also learned that part of this process was learning to let go of expectations, as they often lead to disappointments. I started to take life as it came, accepting that the journey has bright days and cloudy days, and that storms can be embraced. It is in these stormy times when some of the best lessons are learned.

When the unexpected happens

Some storms arrive without warning. While I was on my journey of self-awareness, in 2018, my beautiful, vital mother was diagnosed with two types of incurable cancer. I had to refocus. It was not about me now but about her. I quit my job to become a caregiver for the woman who meant everything to me. It was not so difficult to take a break from work as my passion for it was diminishing by the day. I left without regret, and was instead cheered that I could be closer to my mother and experience a new, life-changing stage in my transformation journey. Things happen for a reason, I thought.

My mother raised me, her only daughter, as a single woman. We were closely connected to each other. Moving abruptly from a hectic working life to becoming a full-time caregiver changed my life completely; no more fancy dinners out, no more travel and social events. My routine changed from high heels and suits to early mornings at hospitals in casual jeans. My world was getting smaller by the day. My conversations were not about targets and revenues anymore but about medical reports, emergency admissions at hospitals, sleepless nights, deep emotional conversations about chemotherapy that resulted in abundant tears. I woke up in fear and went to bed in fear; fear of not having control over the situation; fear of not being able to achieve my new singular objective of keeping my mother alive.

I was hoping for a miracle. The pressure of having to make decisions about someone else's life was devastating. What if I accepted a therapy that did not work? Or accepted medical examinations that would be unbearable for her?

I found myself on an emotional roller coaster. One moment we were celebrating positive medical results and the next we were drenched in sadness because the chemotherapy did not work. We often cried together. It is tough to see your own mother sliding backwards, then to witness her fear of leaving behind her only daughter and granddaughter, holding on desperately to the hope of living just a little bit longer.

In the midst of her emotions, I found myself struggling to find the balance I needed while dealing with the fluctuating emotions so understandable for a terminally ill patient. They say that when cancer hits you it also hits your loved ones. I did not want to accept that her life would end. This fear of loss kept my fighting spirit engaged. I was my mother's strength and inspiration, stimulating her to keep fighting and to believe in a healthy future. Positivity and faith until the end, I thought.

I researched causes of cancer and how to prevent it. I collected information and discussed my findings with specialists. Once, a doctor thought I was a medical professional; such was my ease and familiarity with medical terminology. I learned that our lifestyle has a great impact on our health. Our nutrition and the way we manage stress levels both have enormous impact on our physical condition. I learned that letting go of resentment can have a miraculous healing effect. Through all of this, I was inspired to look at myself differently; to look at myself as a soul searching for life's purpose. I began to feel the need to make a difference in people's lives. Taking my mother by her hand to help her feel safe through this difficult period had brought me a step further in my transition to my new life.

Although caretaking was time-consuming and emotional, I decided to enrol at the Academy for the Art of Living, to seek a post-graduate degree as a holistic vitality and lifestyle specialist, pulling together the three aspects of myself described at the Academy: me as a person, as a coach and as an entrepreneur.

I knew I might be taking on too much, trying to clear too many hurdles, but my developing belief in myself reminded me that I was a strong woman who could depend on faith to move me forward. The universe – and God, if you are a religious – guide us provided we give that higher power the space to manifest its plans for us.

I created a Divine space for the universe to give me the wisdom, the strength and the energy to accomplish all I had taken on. Yes, it was difficult, and I again became a juggler trying to keep so many balls in the air, but my power came through willingness and the right mindset. I learned to let go of fear and not to block myself, to accept moments of failure, for they would make me stronger and keep the fire burning to accomplish my goals.

I woke up every day, grateful for having my mother alive and for the gift of life and wisdom. I learned to express gratitude for what has yet to come, knowing that the Divine power sometimes works in mysterious ways. I started a healing process of forgiveness for all that was wrong in my past, recognising that parents make mistakes and that mine did the best they could given their abilities and knowledge. As long as we care, I believe our unconditional love for our parents will help us to let go of the past. In this process, I also accepted that nothing lasts forever, that parents are here for a limited time. I accepted that miracles do not always happen. As a child, I used to say that I would never survive the loss of my mother. But human beings are continuously growing emotionally and spiritually. We find strength and power beyond what we can imagine.

When my mother finally lost her fight, I was devastated and felt lost, but she had spoken wise words that will play in my head until the end of my time on Earth: 'Enjoy every day of your life. Life is so short, before you know, the light is turned off.'

This care-giving period was part of my transformation process and afforded me the wisdom of choosing how to live my life in harmony with my intrinsic values. Letting go of the gold medal for second-place silver makes me happier. How important is a life full of stress and discomfort, given the briefness of the time we are afforded?

I became conscious that life is too short to spend much time worrying about the future. Instead, I remembered my mother's wise words and decided to live today, not worrying about tomorrow because it may never come. As for my career, I now occasionally coach people who are interested in creating a better version of themselves, and who want to live a better life both physically and emotionally. I accepted a job where I was able to help entrepreneurs realise their dreams to start their own businesses, and later I became an advisor, coaching unemployed people to find their way back into the workplace.

Am I still struggling with uncertainty? You bet. Childhood experiences do not vanish so simply, but I have now learned that our bodies reflect our unspoken emotions. By recognising the signs, you can address the source and heal yourself. I am still not ready to jump from the highest springboard, but I go for the middle way that resonates with who I am and which best suits my nature.

I feel privileged to have developed a mission: to be that ship that will take people to a safe harbour despite the storm. I believe I am here to fulfil a human-centric role, helping people in their search for abundant happiness, and grateful for any contribution I can give to the world.

If you find yourself facing signs that move you from within, dare to listen to yourself. Trust in that voice so that belief in yourself can lead you from simple change to profound transition. When you open yourself and allow your supreme power to guide you, you may notice a refined stream of trust. This confidence will be your best buddy to take you through this journey of transition, often full of surprises.

My sincere hope is that I have inspired you not to be frightened when events or your own inner voice give you signs that you are facing transitions. Fear and failure are always around trying to overrule our feelings and lessen our faith in ourselves. But through perseverance and determination you can overcome your fears. You should be grateful for this experience as it provides an opportunity to gain insights that will enrich you and help you to do better in this world.

Honouring the Divine Mother is Honouring Yourself

By Amanda Winwood

Honouring the Divine Mother is Honouring Yourself

*"Loving my mother gave me freedom
to love life…and myself."*

Earth Mother

*Have confidence – Be Brave in this Wide World
Fear nothing; for fear is a canker which gnaws at
The core and damages the fruit, but fill your heart
With love, for love is at the root of all Life's Joy and Mystery*

This poem was shared with me by my mother on March 28, 1978, just over three months before my 16th birthday and two months before she died. These words have, in an uncertain world, been an anchor, rooting me to a truth that has remained unchanged throughout a life that now spans nearly six decades. At a time of immense uncertainty with a pandemic igniting fear in every strata of humanity, I hold my mother's words close to my heart. Replacing fear with love makes life, whatever it holds, a place of peace both within and beyond me.

These words have been at my core since I was young and resonate even more now I am older. We all need an anchor in life to give us the strength and resilience we need to move forward. I am no longer the young woman my mum urged to "tend my talents lovingly" and I read the words now with a wisdom I did not have at 16. This is the purpose of my story – to encourage you to honour yourself, be kind to yourself and others, be brave and know that you will always be loved, by many. But to love yourself is at the heart of growth. This has been my biggest lesson throughout my life.

So, let us start with the story of the Mother because in truth that is where you start to be defined. I believe that every human being is a book waiting to be written when they are born. At birth, we are a pure, blank page but even at that stage, our experience pre-birth will influence our story. Were we wanted and nurtured while we were in the womb? As an intrinsic part of our mother's body, how do we relate to that time?

My mother was beautiful and could light up a room when she walked into it. She shone with an innate intelligence and a sense of interest and fun that made her appealing to both men and women, and she was always the life and soul of the party. Some people said that I reminded them of her, which I found difficult to accept as my sister, Kate, looked more like her than I did. I understand now that we may take on different elements of parents and people. My sister has our mother's dark Italian beauty but I share her outlook on life. She taught me not just about resilience and living my truth, but she endowed me with a passion for life and also art, wellbeing and herbs and flowers.

Our mother was beautiful, but she was also sad and dissatisfied with what most people would have regarded as a privileged life. She had all the trimmings and trappings that generally went with an upper middle-class background and so did we. Yet even as a child I remember her searching for something that would make her feel more content, fulfilled and happy.

Maybe the true story for my mother and me started in 1975 with a chance meeting on a beach in Spain between my mother and an artist, Jack Rutherford. The events that unfolded from there shaped all of our lives and helped define me and my sister as children and also the women we became.

We are all just memory maps and what we experience when we are young shapes our view and passage through life. It can be a blessing or a burden, but we always have a choice of how to look at life and how to live it. When we are young, we are blissfully unaware of how we are affected by everything we touch, see and experience. Often, we pack everything neatly away in the suitcase of our mind. There it sits, often like a time bomb, waiting for the moment when a trigger will make it burst open and old feelings, hurts, anxieties, and traumas fly out.

I still remember the exact moment when I found my mum in our kitchen with Jack. Too close to be just friends, they leapt apart as I walked through the door. My dad was out chopping wood at the time. I was 13 and old enough to understand that what I had seen was not right. 'Why don't you go and help my dad chop wood?' I suggested to Jack.

That evening my parents hosted a party with an exhibition of Jack's work in our home. The great and the good of the Cheshire set arrived and were served wine and a selection of the cocktail foods that were the essence of the 1970s – cheese and pineapple on sticks, sausage rolls and vol au vents. Kate and I were allowed to stay up and help serve people early on. Several of Jack's paintings sold; abstract concepts in bold, vivid oils, of landscapes with wizened olive trees. My dad bought two himself. I have them now as later he could not bear the sight of them and they were locked away in an attic; a reminder of betrayal.

Jack left just a week after the exhibition and our lives returned to normal. Some months after his stay, Mum took me and Kate to stay with her parents, our much-loved Granny and Grandpa. They lived on the outskirts of Bath in Woolley and I loved the little bedroom that was mine whenever I stayed there. We had all had dinner and Kate was asleep in the room she was sharing with my mum when I was awoken by shouting and crying. I crept outside of my room and at the end of the corridor saw my grandfather, shouting, 'You slut!' at my mum as my granny wept. I ran up the corridor and shouted, 'Don't call my mummy names'. My grandpa just looked at me, then at my mum, and stamped into his living room, slamming the door. I remember asking my granny not to cry and hugging her.

Mum told me to go back to bed and then some time later she came into my room and told me that she was in love with Jack, and that she planned to live in Spain with him and take me and Kate with her. 'Does Daddy know?' I asked.

'No sweetheart, he doesn't. I am going to tell him, but I need you to keep it a secret with me.'

Six weeks it took. For six weeks I held "the secret," knowing that the life I was living was a lie. I still remember sitting with my dad and mum in the kitchen when they told me that they were going to try to work things out. They didn't. The dreams that my mum had of taking us to live in Spain crumbled like ash as the viciousness of a divorce ensued.

Kate and I now talk of how we were affected by the arguments and deceit we witnessed. Our lives were turned upside down and our normality tumbled around us like shattered glass. It was painful, sad and left scars that took a long time to heal.

We always have choices to make in life. Having gone through my own divorce, I have learned the hard way. I have often asked myself, what is the right thing to do? Do you set aside your own life and self and put your children first, even if it means living a lie? Or do you take a risk and live your truth? I know now that there is no right or wrong, there are simply choices and outcomes.

My mum was judged. Kate and I judged her, people we loved and trusted judged her. I felt embarrassed by our "hippie" mother. We loved and hated her at the same time and chose to take our anger out by often refusing to spend more than the minimum amount of time we could with her. I now know how much this must have hurt her, but it took a long time to forgive her and understand how painful it had been for her to leave without us.

Life has a funny way of repeating itself. We think it teaches us lessons, but sometimes we remember the lessons too late. I too, walked away from my seemingly perfect marriage and experienced much the same as my mum did. My two beautiful daughters experienced the same as Kate and I did. It has also taken them years to really understand and forgive.

It is an incredible thing to experience judgement and rejection from people you love and care for. After my divorce, my Christmas card list evaporated. Some of my "friends" would literally cross the street to avoid me or refuse to say hello. Great times drinking wine and enjoying dinner parties, and holidays with friends and family all became things of the past.

I felt like a leper and no one bothered to ask me what had happened. I lost all my confidence, suffered with anxiety and depression, and withdrew into a deep shell. There were times when the only thing that kept me functioning was my love for my two girls. In the midst of it all though, I learned that I didn't need a big group of so-called friends. I have friends with whom I share truth and compassion, and with whom love is at the core. Real friends are people who tell you their thoughts, having taken the time to try to understand first.

Our mum had nothing, in a material sense. She chose to live a life in Spain with a talented but impoverished artist. When she came back to see us, we stayed with her, with friends who still spoke to her, in houses in woods and in camper vans. On the contrary, Kate and I were spoiled by both our dad and our grandparents, with holidays, clothes, a pony, a beautiful home; everything that we could want for as teenagers except for hugs, love and time shared with our mum.

About two months before my 16th birthday, Mum came over from Spain and we went to see her at a friend's home. We later found out that she was over to finalise the divorce with Dad. That day was a pivotal moment for me. Mum looked tired and sad. She asked me to go for a walk with her and as we passed through the orchard at the back of the house, the scent from the apple blossoms drifted around us. She told me she had been for some tests at the hospital and needed to go in for some more in two weeks' time. Something deep inside me shifted.

As we stood in the orchard with the sunshine dappling through the trees around us, I felt all the animosity and anger I had toward my mum dispel. I felt my love for her brimming up and as we held each other, we shared how much we loved each other, and we cried. As we walked back towards the house, holding hands, I felt something inevitable sit with me. I just knew that this could possibly be one of the last times I would spend with my mum. I cried all the way home when Dad drove us away from her. Three weeks later, she died. The last time I saw her was in hospital, weak but still with her beautiful smile.

I learned from this, albeit much later, that I cannot choose the course of other people's lives. I cannot blame other people for how I live my own life. My mother's words resonate: 'We are an amalgam of all those who have touched us and those who have touched them.' It is true. It is what we choose to absorb and what we choose to leave behind that is important. Fear, anger and regret are our bitter enemies. I learned on that day in spring, in my 16th year, in an apple-scented orchard, to allow my heart to be filled with compassion and love rather than hurt and blame.

I went off the rails for a time just after my mum's death. I was a rebel and I found my dad's way controlling. I partied excessively, sought love and affection from a succession of boyfriends and became something of a lost soul. The turning point came one night when my dad picked me up from a party and started to shout at me in the car. I shouted back and he tried to hit me, so I jumped out of the moving car and rolled into a ditch. He stopped the car and hauled me out of the ditch and into the car. I sobbed all the way home. However, when I woke up the next day I decided that I wouldn't accept this anymore.

It was a defining moment. I felt scared, shocked and liberated all at the same time, not to mention physically sick. It was a turning point in our relationship and in my life. I have never been able to deal with injustice or bullying and have learned that honest and open conversations can often prevent this. I made a brave attempt to put myself in Dad's shoes. I don't condone how he behaved, but I began to understand how betrayal by someone he loved had made him feel. I learned that we all make mistakes along the way: we will be hurt, we will love, and we will lose people we love. I also learned that kindness to yourself and others, seeking to understand rather than judge, are gifts to hold for life.

Mother Earth
My love for my mother extends into my love for life and Mother Earth. Mum and I shared a passion for the creative, for yoga, for simple joys in life such as herbs and flowers and all things alternative. These interests that she shared with me at a young age have created my own passion for this beautiful Earth upon which we walk, interact and grow.

This has influenced everything I do through my own business, Made for Life, working with herbs and flowers to create organic skincare, and with people and spas to enable therapists to welcome people going through cancer. I have learned that to be healthy, we need to relate to this beautiful planet that we are inextricably linked to; our compassion must extend to fellow humans and beyond, to the very Earth we tread upon.

The Earth needs to be nurtured and we should think about how our actions may achieve this. Without its abundance we have nothing. When you fall in love with nature and its beauty, you honour another mother. Not the person who gave birth to you, but that which gave you the space to be born, to live and to grow. Our relationship with Mother Earth is both fragile and strong, but when we focus on this connection and try to understand how it supports our growth, we grow stronger, too.

My relationship with Earth grows stronger still. I have put down some roots in Spain, right in the heart of Catalunya. In July 2014, I remarried and in 2017, my husband, Geoff, and I travelled on his Harley Davidson through Spain. We fell in love with this land, with its sweeping landscapes and mountains, and with the warmth of both the sunshine and the people here who have a love of artisan living. When I wake up in our 12th century farmhouse, I listen to the sound of birdsong and walk out with a cup of tea, to just sit and enjoy the peace and beauty of the vineyards that surround us. I feel the life in the walls of this building and the energy here soothes and nourishes us.

As I look back on my life so far, I see it reflected in the seasons. Spring is a time of birth and growth. Trees and flowers burst into life and their beauty is inspiring. Leaves unfurl and blossoms bloom. It is a time of creation, innocence and simple beauty. In our own springtime, we are blessed with beauty, but we often don't see it.

Summer is the time of fruition, providing us with the food source and nutrients that we need. In the summer of our lives, we have children who are our own "fruits." They reflect how we care for them, in the same way that a garden in the summer will reflect the way in which it has been lovingly tended.

Autumn may reflect our twilight years, but it is too often seen as a sad season. I see it as a time of potential liberation; an opportunity to shed our worries like the leaves drifting from a tree.

Winter, of course, is our final season. Rather than simply a time when we become cold in death, it can be regarded as a valuable period of quietness and peace. In winter, nature gently rests in order to evolve. Things slow down and some plants die and return to the earth, but some will return in the spring.

When we endow our time to nurture the earth, it can be in simple everyday acts, as well as great schemes. We can choose to simply catch our breath and walk in a park, aware of the sounds and scents that surround us, or we can hatch a bigger plan to limit our waste – it all makes a difference. When we become touched by nature, we find more of an understanding of how it supports us as a species.

As humans, our beliefs define us. My belief is that we will return to the earth and become part of something beyond humanity. I also believe that there is a beauty in all the seasons. It is how we use the seasons of our life that matters.

Divine Mother

In my mother's poem, she refers to keeping faith with God and with myself, for that is God within me. We all have different views on spirituality, faith and God. When I practice mindfulness or Reiki, either as part of my work or in my own practice with retreat guests who visit us in Spain, I feel connected spiritually to the Divine. It is a life force deep within us all. It may be intuition or our inner spirit, but I know that it is a love that flows from somewhere deep within. In the words of my mother,

her love for me is as constant as the sun. My love for others is the same. Our spirituality and beliefs come from our parents and those before them, it grows from a space deep within. When you open your heart to the Divine, you open yourself to energy both outside and within. At the core is love, for yourself and for others. In my mother's words:

The flower of your youth is Blossoming
Unfolding its petals to the sun as a Maiden to
A Lover with that mixture of Eagerness and
Restraint most natural and Becoming

Have confidence – Be Brave in this Wide World
Fear nothing; for fear is a canker which gnaws at
The core and damages the fruit, but fill your heart
With love, for love is at the root of all Life's Joy and Mystery
Remember you are an amalgam of all those
who have touched you, and those who have touched them
– ad infinitum
But at the centre of all that lies the Essence that is you

Be true to that Self; keep bright its flame as a hallowed Shrine
For nothing should tarnish it.
Keep faith with God, and with Yourself which is God within You

Remember to tend lovingly those talents with which you are endowed
For they are a sacred trust and their core will amply reward you.

Remember you are the lovely and gifted young woman we discern
Both because of me and in spite of me
But that my love for you is as Constant as the Sun.

Write Your Own Story

By Mary Ellen Sanger
Writing facilitator and author

None of us is without a story. And none of us is without a unique, interesting, *unusual* story that others could learn from, be inspired by, or even use as a seed to change the world. Even if you are writing for yourself, and expect never to share your writing, asking yourself questions to start shaping a story results in a re-discovery of moments and feelings that can help you to better understand yourself – past and present. Writing our stories can also be immensely healing, as it has been for several of the writers included in this book.

The act of moving your memories to the page can be deeply transformational. When we coax stories from inside our bodies and minds to the blank page *now*, we can examine our past in a way that we may not have been ready for *then*. This kind of writing, challenging as it may be, is rewarding beyond measure as we discover facets of ourselves and develop new perspective around incidents in our lives.

What follows is a series of small steps that can help you move toward writing your own story. It doesn't matter how you do them, as long as you commit to doing as many steps as you can to get your writing "mojo" flowing. If you've never written before – and even if you have – you may be surprised to read what emerges when you invite your muse and your memory to sit together for a creative while!

How do I begin?

Intuitive healer and coach Velleda Dobrowolny worked with the writers in this book to guide them through an "intention-setting" that would set them on the path to discovery. She says, 'Like a small seed contains an entire plant or tree, so your intention has the power to manifest the reality you wish for yourself.' Before you start to write, you may want to engage with this process, as described by Velleda, to create your own intention for your story.

1. Close your eyes

Reflect for a few minutes on your life, acknowledging the many lessons gained as well as the missed opportunities, the successes as well as the trials and tribulations you have gone through.

+ Consider what you have been able to give, and what you were blessed to receive from others.
+ Reflect on the relationships that have been especially meaningful to you.
+ After you have reflected, take notes for a few minutes. Write down anything that stands out for you. Pay attention to your feelings as you write about the various events.

2. Now, ask yourself:

What was the main turning point in my life? What supported me to break free? To find my own voice? To understand my self-worth, or to manifest my own power?

+ Reflect and write.

3. Consider gratitude

If you haven't already, identify for what or to whom you are most grateful; who or what has supported you most in life?

✦ Reflect and write.

4. Formulate your intention

That is, why do you want to share your life's story with others? What is the one message you want to pass on? Reflect and write for a few minutes.

✦ At the end of your reflections you will have a complete statement of your intention. Keep it brief, so you can remember it easily. Here are some examples:

"I want to write the story of my life to encourage people to honour themselves, be kind to themselves and others, to be brave and to know that they will always be loved, by many. But to love yourself is at the heart of growth. This has been my biggest learning throughout my life."

"What I'd like to share is my experience with death. Death teaches us how to live. If we love, forgive, give thanks and practice compassion throughout our life, we will die well and live well. For love is the foundation for life, in this body and beyond."

Trust yourself. You know your life better than anyone. Your story has value: You spent a lifetime building it! You are a writer once you put your pen to paper. You've written plenty in your life, but you probably haven't always called it "writing." Now, you are going to call yourself a writer and begin. Even if you have written before, the following exercises will help enrich your "memory muscle" to find focus and direction for the story you will write now.

Okay, I have my intention. Now what?

Start by honouring your story, by making the space and creating the time for your story to emerge.

Do you have a special space in your home or community where you feel safe and comfortable? A special journal to write in – Lined? Unlined? Graph paper? Handmade? – the perfect pen? YES! You are going to start with a PEN – something "different" happens when you step away from the screen and use your own script to put things down on paper. Purple ink? Gel? Fountain? Music in the background? A scented candle? Warm socks and a cosy sweater? Enough light? Make the moment sensual, as you are going to be calling on your senses as you dive into memory.

Invite your muse to sit with you.

Now that you are comfortable and serene… You will write.

Keep your intention close. You can refer to it for inspiration and direction whenever you may need a reminder.

Now you are going to generate some specific, concrete memories. Number your blank page from 1 to 50. Give yourself a timed 30 minutes to write a list of 50 memories from your life. You don't have to worry about chronology or detail – you can write one sentence or even one word that evokes that memory for you. Keep going. Keep your pen moving. This is meant to be a "stream of consciousness" exercise that limbers your memory and pulls things out that you may not dwell on every day. They can be small: "My first kitten." Or larger: "When I went away to Spain."

Think of sensory memories such as the ways things smelled, tasted, sounded, felt and appeared. Sunlight through trees. The acrid smell of smoke. The first time you tasted papaya. The feel of your toes in your favorite fuzzy slippers. The crashing sound from that car accident.

Now what?

Now that you have generated a long list of memories, go back through them and highlight four or five that have the most "energy" or "fit" best with the intention you have set for yourself. It is not unusual, at this point, to amend your intention if another perspective has emerged.

Use those memories to write, quickly again, for 30 minutes on each and without trying to "write well", creating a longer, more detailed memory full of as many senses as you can pull in. Keep your pen moving on the paper. Write one story. Then another. And a third, fourth, fifth. Keep those senses evident. What does your past smell like? Taste like?

This is a very personal stage. You are writing you. Don't give up on yourself.

And then?

By now you have words flying from your pen. By now, you are getting the hang of this writing thing.

It's time to try to respond to some prompts that will pull you into your story even more. You can move to the screen if this is more comfortable to you now. Or keep going with your favorite pen in your journal. These are still "stream of consciousness" pieces, a kind of preparatory canvas for putting your story together. Your earlier intention setting is landing on the page now.

Try starting with these statements:

My first memory is...

A secret I've never told is...

Now that I'm older I know...

I did my best but...

I knew I should have...

The first time I...

Do as many as you like, or make up your own. The strength of this writing prompt is in not thinking too much. Not forcing yourself to write well or correctly. The strength is in allowing your mind to flow through thoughts without editing, without what writing guru, Natalie Goldberg, calls "monkey mind." Just keep writing and don't stop. Don't let the monkey edit you, yet.

Put it all together

My biggest tip for writing your story? Sit down and do it! By now you've done the most challenging work of digging into your own memories, the rich history that is yours alone.

As you start to put your written fragments together as a full story on the page, you can think about "craft" angles around writing: timeline, perspective, tense, voice, what to include and not. Write from your heart and worry about craft later. If you keep close to your intention and write your truth, you'll be pleased with the final product. Even Hemingway had an editor... that is for another day!

Congratulations. This kind of deep writing gives us a free and readily available resource for taking care of ourselves, for releasing pent-up emotional stresses, and helping us cope with life traumas. We may encounter meaning in the events of our lives that heals and moves us toward greater emotional health.

Happy writing!

What are YOUR words?

Authors' Invitation

The authors of this book continue to hold space for each other as part of an online community. We see it is a space where we allow ourselves to be nourished and encouraged, to ask questions and to learn from each other. We hang out on a private Facebook page and you are invited to join our "soul conversations" at *Creating Purpose Through Passion*.

If you want to find out what other activities and events we are hosting, check out **www.soul-luxury.com**

Our journeys are connected… We Are Every Woman!

Acknowledgements

We, the collective group of authors, are grateful to each other for the supportive space that has been held with immense love, compassion and gratitude. We have embraced this book journey together and have found deep comfort, insight and strength in the process of writing our chapters. We are blessed and privileged to be a part of this book project, and trust our unique journeys will unfold… exactly as they are meant to.

Claudia, lioness of light, thank you for attracting us all in and allowing us to grow. You are the beating heart of *I Am Every Woman* and you have graciously, with boundless patience and endless encouragement, allowed every one of us to shine in our own truth and presence. You have created and bestowed the gift of self-connection to burgeon within each of us.

Thank you, Mary Ellen, you have been a treasure of light. Your professional editing and ongoing guidance were always infused with so much compassion for each author's unique journey. And your creative talent gifted us with a beautiful cover design that shares the power and beauty of *I Am Every Woman*.

Velleda, thank you for setting us on the right path with a very special intention-setting workshop.

Sarah, you have captured the collective journey so well in your foreword, and we have cherished your valuable input and guidance throughout this amazing journey.

Corinna, we love our book's title!

Karin, thank you for harvesting your gift to create fun coffee cups, integrating the group Coffee Morning gatherings.

We are extremely grateful to the Marketing Committee (Anja, Christine, Claudia, Elodie, Justine, Karin, Susan) for so generously investing the necessary time and effort to pull it all together. We know this was not an easy task with 15 women involved!

Dear reader, we thank you for picking up this book. May the light of love, health and abundance be with you.

Elodie Baran	Sharan Patel
Justine Clement	Stella Photi
Susan Devine	Uma Prajapati
Christine Hale	Julia Record
Anja Loetscher	Claudia Roth
Liliana Martins	Astrid Salas
Karin Mlaker	Amanda Winwood
Louisa Pantameli	

Start Your Story Here